In Days to Come

In Days to Come

FROM ADVENT TO EPIPHANY

GEORGE H. DONIGIAN

UPPER ROOM BOOKS®
NASHVILLE

IN DAYS TO COME: FROM ADVENT TO EPIPHANY
Copyright © 2017 by George H. Donigian
All rights reserved.

At the time of publication all websites referenced in this book were valid. However, due to the fluid nature of the Internet some addresses may have changed, or the content may no longer be relevant.

Scripture quotations not otherwise identified are taken from the New Revised Standard Version Bible © 1989, Division of Christian Education of the National Council of the Churches of Christ in the United States of America. Used by permission. All rights reserved.

Scripture quotations from THE MESSAGE. Copyright © by Eugene H. Peterson 1993, 1994, 1995, 1996, 2000, 2001, 2002. Used by permission of NavPress Publishing Group.

Scripture quotations designated NASB are taken from the New American Standard Bible®, Copyright © 1960, 1962, 1963, 1968, 1971, 1972, 1973, 1975, 1977, 1995 by The Lockman Foundation. Used by permission. (www.Lockman.org)

ISBN: 978-0-8358-1713-4 (PRINT); 978-0-8358-1714-1 (KINDLE); 978-0-8358-1715-8 (EPUB)

Printed in the United States of America

Contents

Gratitude for Gifts Along the Way

Preparation for Christmas brings to mind the giving and receiving of gifts. Some gifts surprise, delight, and stir up joy. Some gifts evoke disappointment, while others evoke odd combinations of emotion and perhaps the question, *What were they thinking?*

We receive gifts, and we give to others. Among the knick-knacks I keep near my desk is a gift for my sixteenth birthday from my mother. It remains in the original packaging: a die-cast scale model of an Oldsmobile Toronado made by Corgi Toys in Great Britain. "You said you wanted a car for your birthday," she remarked. Funny—though not what I had hoped to receive.

Writing a book also brings thoughts of gifts along the way. I am certainly thankful in the present for the love and support of my wife, Mary Teasley, and our growing family.

I think of others along the journey of life who were gifts at the right time and to whom I have not expressed my gratitude. Some are lifelong friends. Others showed up for a season.

Don Saliers—with gratitude for a friendship that matured over the years since seminary days.

Deb Kazanjian Giragosian—with gratitude for family connections and history.

David L. Powell, Karen Holley Horrell, Jeanne Oakes Shipp, Keith M. Parsons, and Michael Paul Farr—college and university friends who challenged me to do better.

Franklin Dotts—for his confidence in hiring me to work as a children's curriculum editor at The United Methodist Publishing House.

Catherine E. Bonner—mystical poet and friend who showed up much too infrequently and disappeared too soon.

For these and many other people, I am ever grateful.

I am thankful to Joanna Bradley of Upper Room Books who asked if I had any ideas for Advent books. I remain grateful for Rita Collett, whose vocation as an editor wholeheartedly embraces the need for the right thought, the right word, and the right punctuation. Many thanks for corporate patience while I wrote this material on a tight deadline.

To you who are reading this book, I am also thankful that together we journey in faith, discovering more of the depths of God's love.

Experiencing Book and Author

Advent calendars help us mark time as we move toward Christmas. Advent calendars may be simple or ornate. Usually made from heavy paper, flaps open to reveal an image for the day. More ornate Advent calendars are wooden with cubicles for users to open and mark the days. The first Advent calendars highlighted religious symbols and traditions that pointed toward Christmas. Today Advent calendars may show cartoon characters or cars, photos of nature or technological devices, in addition to religious symbols. Most of the commercially prepared calendars begin on December 1, though beginning on the first Sunday of Advent seems more appropriate.

As a child myself and then years later with my own children, I enjoyed opening the windows of the Advent calendar to see the symbol or reminder of faith. Sometimes the representations fostered meaningful conversations with my mother about Christian discipleship. Sometimes we unpacked the symbolism, for example, when one calendar showed a boat. I learned then that a ship represented the church.

Advent calendars do more than mark the passage of time; they allow symbols and signs of God's love and God's differing gifts to surprise us as we move toward Christmas. As you read this book, you will see that I have numbered the meditations in a reverse numerical order. I think of these meditations as an Advent calendar. The first meditation is number 24; the meditations count down from that first meditation of Advent to the last meditation. As you read them, you will also see that, unlike most Advent calendars, the meditations continue through the season of Christmas and end with Epiphany. Each week includes an introduction and four meditations. You may choose to read the introduction on a Sunday and then read the meditations on a Monday-Tuesday, Thursday-Friday plan or as they fit your schedule during this busy season. An optional approach would be to read the opening antiphon of each week on day 1 and spend some time pondering its words. On day 2 a reader would read the introduction, then on days 3–6, the four meditations would follow. Finally, on day 7, the questions for the week would allow you to reflect on your reading, prepare for a group discussion if you are involved in such, and simply rest and reflect. I hope that each portion—antiphon, week introduction, meditations, and reflection questions will help you grow as a follower of Christ and to practice the disciplines of the spiritual journey.

Each year of my childhood, my family celebrated Christmas on December 25 *and* January 6. We called December 25 "American Christmas." We would attend a Christmas Eve service at a local church. On December 25 we opened Christmas gifts from Santa Claus and one another. Christmas carols and songs played in the background throughout the day. My family also held an open house on Christmas afternoons, and the hours for those gatherings expanded. Friends began arriving for our family's last Christmas open house around noon, and the last of the visitors left at midnight.

On January 6 my family celebrated Armenian Christmas, known also in the Armenian tradition as Theophany. The

Christmas traditions of the Armenian Apostolic Orthodox Church differ from our American celebration in that Armenians celebrate the nativity and the baptism of Christ at the same time. By January 1, my non-Armenian friends were commenting and asking when my family would remove its Christmas decorations. I learned that many of them took down their decorations on Christmas Day or on December 26. How odd that seemed to me, and how odd our notions seemed to them!

Armenian Christmas traditions center around church and family time. The church recommends fasting for the week prior to January 6. According to one Armenian tradition, the Virgin Mary went into labor after eating spinach. Armenian observance thus includes a spinach dish on Christmas Eve, a tradition my family observed on an irregular basis.

I still like to connect the two Christmas traditions. Celebrating the two Christmases changes my sense of time. I do not have to stop listening to Christmas music on December 24 simply because commercial interests want us to prepare for Valentine's Day. I can continue to enjoy the music and the decorations of Christmas and reflect on the journey of the magi, as well as the escape of the Holy Family to Egypt. After this event comes a gradual movement into the calendar's flow of Ordinary Time and then Ash Wednesday.

Lingering in the longer season of Christmas gives a deeper sense of wonder and awe concerning the Incarnation—the basic task of the church calendar. We begin the Christian year in Advent with a sense of expectation and hope. We prepare to celebrate God's gift in Jesus Christ. We come to a sense of fulfillment at Christmas and discover a renewed sense of awe and praise at the news of Jesus' birth. We continue to reflect with a sense of wonder as the church year moves to Epiphany and the remembrance of the magi's visit.

In Days to Come offers devotional meditations that carry us from Advent to Epiphany, from the season of expectation to the season of fulfillment and mission. As you read and reflect on the writings, I hope you will experience a slowing down and an expansion of the seasonal rhythm.

Within strong liturgical traditions, people sing or chant antiphons in response to a psalm. An antiphon is "a verse or a series of verses sung as a prelude or conclusion to some part of the service." Each week's meditations grow from the "O Antiphons." The title of each one begins with the vocative *O*. Each antiphon is a name of Christ, one of his characteristics mentioned in scripture. They are as follows:

O Sapientia (O Wisdom)
O Adonai (O Lord)
O Radix Jesse (O Root of Jesse)
O Clavis David (O Key of David)
O Oriens (O Dayspring)
O Rex Gentium (O King of the nations)
O Emmanuel (O With Us Is God)

The "O Antiphons" are sung or recited at the vesper services from December 17–23, the last week of Advent in the liturgy of the Roman Catholic and Anglican traditions, originating in the fifth century in the Latin language of the church. Their focusing designations come from the prophet Isaiah and grow from attributes of the promised Messiah. In this book the titles will help us pause and see Advent-Christmas-Epiphany with deeper eyes of faith. (*The United Methodist Hymnal* includes all the "O Antiphons" after the hymn "O Come, O Come, Emmanuel.")

The meditations will reflect on Bible passages that anticipate the coming Messiah. Isaiah and Micah describe mission and ministry. From the Gospel of Luke we hear the songs of Elizabeth and Mary. As we move through Christmas, we also hear Zechariah's prophecy. Reflection will also take us into consideration of light—the first part of Creation.

I did not limit the meditations to reflection on Bible passages. You will read about seasonal music and art and about writers or composers. I believe that all our creativity can point to a greater awareness of God at work in the world. Our lives in the present build upon the lives of our ancestors—all the sisters and brothers in Christ. W. Paul Jones, in the introduction to his book *An Eclectic Almanac for the Faithful,* describes our need to learn from a greater history: "What we encounter is the creativity and compassion of a God who specializes in making us instruments of the divine vision in spite of ourselves" (page 7). As we intentionally slow down the pace of time from Advent to Epiphany, we will begin to see how God partners with us in the divine vision of love eternal.

As a reader, you know your history and how you came to faith, your participation in church life, and how you practice spiritual disciplines. I have diverse interests. You may learn a smattering about Armenia, jazz, John Wesley, baseball, spiritual practices, and poetry along with reflections on Bible passages and this time of year. My journey of faith has been a winding one that began with my baptism at Saint Gregory the Illuminator Armenian Apostolic Orthodox Church in Philadelphia, Pennsylvania. I eventually moved to confirmation in the Lutheran Church-Missouri Synod before I became part of The United Methodist Church. I have worked as a pastor and a book editor. I also worked on a garbage truck and in a sandpaper factory. (Both of those jobs had their gritty facets.) And in these latter days, I have served as pastor and author. I am the author of several books, including *A World Worth Saving* and *Three Prayers You'll Want to Pray. A World Worth Saving* offers guidance for the season of Lent and also includes stories of heritage, tradition, and transformation. The same description seems appropriate for

Three Prayers, a book that invites readers to a disciplined practice of praying prayers from Dag Hammarskjöld, Reinhold Niebuhr, and Jesus of Nazareth. Thank you for reading this book and for being part of the community of faith as we move forward in these days of hope.

First Week of Advent

O Emmanuel, our King and Lawgiver,
the Expected of the nations and their Savior:
Come and save us, O Lord, our God.

I enjoy the television series *Star Trek* in all its variations: the first series with William Shatner, the later series with Patrick Stewart, and the two spin-offs, *Deep Space Nine* and *Voyager*. The series offers an appealing vision of the future, and I find the assumptions about science and technology made throughout the series fascinating. Some technological advances made in the first two series, such as the digital tablet, have become reality. I look forward to a time when we can transport ourselves across great distances of time and space.

Despite the future orientation of the series, some episodes travel *back* in time and show the potential of a history that could have changed the world. In one such journey into the past, a small mission team from the Starship Enterprise interacted with Samuel Clemens and a young Jack London. In this episode, the "away" team faced the pressure of not changing history's time line. Nothing changed—so much for the wonderful nonreality of television! However, the idea of traveling back in time to meet people and witness particular events intrigues me. So bear with me as we take time to travel backward in time.

Imagine you are a Christian layperson living in Italy in the year 500 CE. You work in fields or manage household affairs. Perhaps you farm, work in a carpentry shop, or bake goods for sale. Your simple and functional clothing does not differ much from that worn in Jesus' time or even in ancient Greece five hundred years before Jesus. Men wore short tunics and shirts. Women wore full-length tunics. Your extended family surrounds you. You enjoy family life. You have children who play and work beside you. You work hard. You hear rumors of wars, but those rumors come from far away and you feel secure. Various warrior tribes, such as the Huns, the Visigoths, or the Vandals are attacking nations. The Empire verges on collapse. With no media reporting, no one knows about the impending collapse. In your spare time, you raise questions about the world; but most of the time you work and talk about community matters and mix in some gossip.

You go to worship. Humanity has not yet put into practice the architectural principles that brought about the great medieval cathedrals. Christmas approaches and with others in the congregation, you join in prayer. You hear a priest proclaim in the Latin language of the church:

O Emmanuel, Rex et legifer noster,
exspectatio Gentium, et Salvator earum:
veni ad salvandum nos, Domine, Deus noster.

O Emmanuel, our King and Lawgiver,
the Expected of the nations and their Savior:
Come and save us, O Lord, our God.

As you worship, maybe this prayer nudges you to think about God's vision of salvation for the world. Perhaps you begin to look beyond the drudgery of daily life and anticipate a future of hope fulfilled. You begin to anticipate the coming of salvation through the Expected One. And we are not so far removed from such hope and desire for salvation.

We perceive and experience many changes between the year 500 and our own time. We sometimes describe our daily work as a grind, but that work generally is not as grueling as was the work of the sixth century. We probably do not live near our extended families today, and the dimensions and boundaries of family life vary greatly from the year 500. Today we learn quickly about events beyond our community, and such news often generates fear. We receive news 24/7, but the tyranny of the news cycle allows for little follow-up reporting on yesterday's big story. Whether we lived in the year 500 or the current year, we share some common points of humanity. Throughout this history, we—along with our ancestors—live with a sense that hope and love will overcome the power of evil.

We go to worship today. Styles of worship are unlike those of the sixth century and diverge from church to church or from various services within a congregation's experience. We may prefer a contemporary style of worship or a contemplative one, a traditional service in a sanctuary or a service set in a coffee house. Our choices for worship continue to point to the desire of our hearts and to the hope and love that God extends.

We continue to anticipate Christmas and the celebration of Jesus' birth, this sacred celebration of Emmanuel—God with us. What do you anticipate this Christmas? What vision do you pray to see fulfilled? As you read this week's meditations and prayers and as you continue the Advent journey toward Christmas, may you experience wonder and awe.

24—A Prophet

We remember that Emmanuel means "God with us." Read Isaiah 2:1-5. The passage begins with words easy to overlook: *In days to come.* Peering into the near future, we see *in days to come* the arrival of the Christmas holiday. We may envision a festival like those in storybooks in which a joyful family gathers in love around a table laden with food and good cheer. Or we may picture a holiday that fulfills our fantasies. Or our holiday vision may embrace a day of service to the homeless or those who live in a memory care unit of a senior living center.

Our vision for Christmas may be less positive or hopeful. We may not have money to fulfill our desires. We may have lost a job or experienced the death of a loved one. We may react to hard times and think *Nothing is changed; nothing will change.* As it was in the beginning, so it always will be.

That cynicism overflowed in me one Advent when, within two months, my mother died, a family member brought legal action against her estate, my research fellowship advisor died, and a friend committed suicide. In the midst of that sad and cynical time, a larger vision of Christmas jolted me from despondent reality to a sense of hope. I developed some new connections, sought emotional and psychological health, and began to pray in varying ways. The words of the Jesus Prayer ("Lord Jesus Christ, have mercy on me") became a close companion as I prayed them over and over and as I rested in that mercy.

When reading Isaiah 2:1-5, the phrase *in days to come* seemed to beg for my attention. *In days to come* points beyond us and our immediate reality, directing us to a broader perspective. The prophet Isaiah surely understands the daily crises of life. Isaiah 1 reminds us that the prophet witnesses the sin of his time. He knows the wicked reality of Judah and the city of Jerusalem. Even so, his perspective remains broad. The everyday obstacles of sin do not block Isaiah's vision for the future. Amid the brokenness surrounding him, Isaiah speaks of the vision when all people will worship in the house of God. The day will come when the world's diverse peoples will meet in peace to companion one another. In that time, people will turn instruments of war and destruction into implements of nurture. In days to come, says Isaiah, people shall learn war no more.

In days to come we will face urgent matters and troubled times. We may feel mired in personal and corporate controversies. We may become dispirited because institutions we once trusted, such as the church, show evidence of possible collapse. People may interpret other signs as indicators of the crumbling of the familiar order. We do not yet see the vision of what will be, but we are becoming witnesses to a new future. In days to come, God will enlarge our awareness and understanding—that of all people—to know that God's ways are not born of our usual human interaction. The time will come when war and rumors of war will not shatter our lives.

In days to come, we will also experience personal happiness, success, and peace, knowing that God intends these gifts for all people. The rhythm of our human condition comes in experiencing desert valleys of hardship and mountain peaks of joy and love. As Christian disciples, no matter our path, we travel with Jesus Christ as our companion.

Read Isaiah 2:1-5 again. As you read and reflect on this passage, ask God for a vision of the *days to come* and ponder how your life reflects this vision. You may choose to imagine Jesus sitting beside you. Invite him to tell you how the following verse connects with your discipleship.

O Emmanuel, our King and Lawgiver,
the Expected of the nations and their Savior:
Come and save us, O Lord, our God.

23 — A Prayer Practice

During the writing of this book, I have been praying the antiphons using a modified form of *lectio divina* (holy reading), an ancient pattern of prayer that prays with a Bible passage. Used primarily in small groups, the *lectio divina* approach to prayer may be tailored for personal devotional guidance. In *lectio divina*, a person reads a short Bible passage aloud to gain basic familiarity with the text. The reader reads the passage a second time posing this question for reflection, "How does this passage touch my life?" After a third reading of the text, the reader responds to another question, "Is this passage inviting me to do something in the next day or so?" Prayer follows a fourth reading of the text.

Before I tell you about my experience with the antiphon, I invite you to try a similar approach. Read this antiphon three times, pausing between the readings. The first reading familiarizes you with the words.

O Emmanuel, our King and Lawgiver,
the Expected of the nations and their Savior:
Come and save us, O Lord, our God.

The second reading offers opportunity to meditate on the words. Does a word or phrase seem to jump out and call for your attention? How does this prayer touch your life?

Read the antiphon a third time. Continue to pay attention to any words or phrases that seem to attract your attention and focus. Ask whether this prayer includes or signals an invitation to do something in the next day or so. After you reflect on this question, pray for further guidance from God. Now take time to pray the antiphon before you continue reading this meditation.

As I prayed this antiphon, the word *lawgiver* attracted my focus. I began to ask why this word and not one of the words that I appreciate more, such as *Emmanuel* or *hope*. *Lawgiver?* I argued with myself and with God. I suggested that *lawgiver* was not the word for me, that my experience of laws and rules and regulations in childhood and adolescence had been sufficient lawgiving for a lifetime, and that I experienced Christ as the liberator from all those rules and regulations.

When I went to Fork Union Military Academy, the first book I received was titled *Rules and Regulations. Army Field Manual 22-5* came next. No, I did not want *lawgiver* to twinkle and attract my notice. Still, *lawgiver* continued in its own curious way to twinkle and demand my attention. I resisted at first, remembering especially the sense of law I received at home and then in the official regulations at Fork Union Military Academy. I began to unpack the meaning of *lawgiver* and found myself moving to an image of Moses atop Mount Sinai. There he receives the law from God. While tradition identifies Moses as the lawgiver, I began again to see God in the role of lawgiver.

I continued to reflect on the antiphon and recalled that Torah, the law, is itself a gift. Consider the circumstances of the twelve tribes: They lived as slaves in Egypt for generations. The royal decrees of pharaoh provided order. Freed from slavery, the people tend toward disorder, evidenced by their panicked approval of the smelting of jewelry to make a golden calf. (See Exodus 32.) Amid disorder, Torah is a gift to bring order out of chaos. I need to remember that Torah offered spiritual and practical guidance for everyday life.

While the idea of the law's restrictions seem to chafe me, that resistance is more the reaction of my inner two-year-old's voice and does not reflect my reality. I voluntarily practice certain spiritual disciplines, including daily Bible reading and reflection, a set time each morning for prayer and journaling, and other practices. Some people would describe these practices as legalities, but I choose to do them. These practices are gifts.

Perhaps these gifts are not what culture associates with Christmas, but they remain gifts nonetheless.

As you have followed this meditation, you may have taken time already today to pray the antiphon. If you have not used the modified *lectio divina* prayer approach, take time to pray the antiphon as described above. What word or words seem to call for your attention? What invitation to deeper discipleship do you hear in response to the prayer? How will this prayer shape your day?

> **God, your love is the force behind Torah. Your love encompasses all, and you bear no grudges in that love. Write your law of love on our hearts, and guide us to see your gifts in wonder and awe today. Amen.**

22—A Counting Song

I look forward to the varied special music during the Advent-Christmas season. I sometimes go on a rant because radio stations play "The Twelve Days of Christmas" in the middle of October rather than waiting until the actual days of Christmas. Despite my rants, the time comes to listen to music that points toward the birth of Jesus, God's gift of incarnation.

For several years I helped with my church's after-school ministry. I began helping in order to learn more about after-school ministries because my job involved developing a resource for these programs. We joined in songs and crafts, played games, learned about the Bible, and discovered ways to do mission and ministry. I eventually tested activity and craft ideas, learning that some activities, while age-appropriate and seemingly right on paper, simply did not work in the setting. I discovered engaging activities; but more than this, I learned about a group of children who ranged in age from kindergarten to sixth grade and whose lives reflected the richness of our urban neighborhood.

The children loved to sing. A guitar player led the singing. Sometimes someone would play a hand drum. Sometimes the children played rhythm instruments. One song the group enjoyed singing at all times of the year was "Children, Go Where I Send Thee," an African-American song attributed to Anonymous. Recorded by artists as different as The Fairfield Four, Kenny Rogers, Mandisa, and REO Speedwagon, this counting song offers a vision that spans the Bible. The lyrics remind me of Jesus' instruction to his disciples: "Children go where I send thee. / How will I send thee?/ I'm going to send thee. . . . "

With those words, the count begins with "I'm going to send thee one by one, /One for the little bitty baby/ born, born, born in Bethlehem." Each stanza adds one more and then counts down so that the final stanza goes like this:

Children go where I send thee. / How will I send thee?/ I'm going to send thee
Twelve by twelve, Twelve for the Twelve Apostles;
Eleven by eleven, Eleven for the eleven singing in heaven;
Ten by ten, Ten for the Ten Commandments;
Nine by nine, Nine for the nine that stood in the line;
Eight by eight, Eight for the eight that stood at the gate;
Seven by seven, Seven for the seven that all went to Heaven;
Six by six, Six for the six that never got fixed;
Five by five, Five for the five that came back alive;
Four by four, Four for the four knocking on the door;
Three by three, Three for the Hebrew children;
Two by two, Two for Paul and Silas;
One by one, One for the little bitty baby,
born in Bethlehem.

As with many songs by Anonymous, versions of the song contain variant wording. I encourage you to listen to several different renditions.* Consider listening first to the version by The Fairfield Four and then listen to another version to hear stylistic adaptations of the song and perhaps to hear a nudge from the Holy Spirit.

People associate this song with Christmas because it refers to the baby born in Bethlehem. The song reminds me that our life in God encompasses much history, a history that moves from the Hebrew children and the Ten Commandments to the missionary journeys of Paul and Silas to the mission and ministry of our own time through our everyday acts of faith. Our story may begin with the baby Jesus, but it continues even beyond us to the generations that follow. So we sing the carols of Christmas and the songs of faith that nurture us and may speak to others.

What songs help you prepare to celebrate the birth of Christ? What songs inspire you to live as a faithful disciple of Christ?

God, Christ came into the world to show us your love. As Christ-followers, we invite you to help us open ourselves so that your love will shine through us to all others. Amen.

21—Vision

Christmas Day seems both far and close to us as we anticipate the holiday. If children are part of our lives, their sense of anticipation makes time feel painfully slow. As adults, we know that the pace of time seems to pick up speed the closer we move toward an anticipated date. We have already witnessed too many Christmas-oriented commercials for consumer goods that we will not buy. We have seen too many reindeer pulling sleighs down hills made of whipped cream and chimneys made of candy. We have received e-mail and snail-mail appeals to support charities and causes. We feel worn down by this dissonance between the birth of Jesus and our cultural consumerism. Amid the crossed wires of Christ and culture, we often forget Isaiah's witness and the vision of God's sovereignty.

Isaiah 2 contains a double-edged prophecy. We first see the vision in which all nations and people come to worship the God of Abraham and Sarah, Isaac and Rebekah, and so on. Isaiah's vision is grounded in an understanding of a God who goes beyond the local fertility cults of the Ancient Near East and beyond visions of deities who, unless worshiped, bring destruction to the land and death to the people. Isaiah speaks of a God who invites all people to worship and, even more, to live with one another in the great diversity of nations. According to Isaiah, the people desire to learn holiness, that God "may teach us his ways and that we may walk in his paths" (2:3). Desire to learn and to live in God's ways will lead people to learn ways of peace instead of war and to "beat their swords into plowshares, and their spears into pruning hooks" (v. 4).

Many people join me in a love for these verses and a deeper consideration of their meaning, but Isaiah's prophecy does not end with a vision of harmony and peace. The prophet anticipates a future that contains judgment. The tone of the passage changes with verse 5's invitation to walk with the Lord. Here comes a demand for a reorientation toward the ways of God rather than the culture adopted by the people of Judah. Notice how Isaiah describes the nation as "filled with idols" and how the people worship their own crafts and deeds: "They bow down to the work of their hands, to what their own fingers have made" (v. 8).

We face those same temptations. Just as the people in Isaiah's time lost sight of God's sovereign love and shifted their allegiance to their own accomplishments, we also begin to think that human accomplishment is all that matters. We believe that success happens through an individual's hard work or financial manipulation, forgetting that many people work together in each success. People tell us stories about a "self-made" millionaire, but each solitary dream or idea depends upon the contributions of many people to become reality. Our consumeristic culture tells us that we alone can create success if we buy the right devices. So much in the culture that surrounds us pulls us into the trap of pride. Isaiah offers a clear response to the seductive pull of pride: "The haughty eyes of people shall be brought low, and the pride of everyone shall be humbled" (2:11).

God invites us to share life together with one another and with God. As we live faithfully in community, we understand that many gifts build community through the grace of God. We also learn new definitions and models of success.

Part of the vision of Christmas for me is that we share in God's larger community in which each individual employs God-given gifts for the sake of the common good out of love for God and one another. As God's love transforms lives, we find that we are part of a community in which justice and mercy embrace. The words of Psalm 85 come to mind: "Steadfast love and faithfulness will meet; / righteousness and peace will kiss each other" (v. 10)—a vision of community that inspires me. May this vision of God's love be one of the gifts you open this Christmas.

> **Christ, our shepherd and savior, you are the hope of all people and nations. Open us to the fresh waves of the Holy Spirit so that we may see new visions of your impact on all the world. Amen.**

*Links to three different versions:
The Fairfield Four < https://www.youtube.com/watch?v=040tPQc8zsg>
Johnny Cash <https://www.youtube.com/watch?v=GH0sjczcg48>
Mary Chapin Carpenter < https://www.youtube.com/watch?v=gtjvmaZs2zc>

Questions for the Week

- What is your experience with "O Antiphons," or are they new to you? Have you read or prayed these prayers at another time?

- Consider all the busyness that surrounds you. What seems most important as you prepare for Christmas?

- As you look toward Christmas, what scheduled activity or tradition seems unnecessary? How could you use that time for faithful acts of service?

- Listen to one of the many versions of "Children, Go Where I Send Thee." What is the song's message to you? Where do you feel that God is sending you?

- What do you believe is God's vision for the world? How does that vision shape your actions?

- Meditation 23 offered a brief introduction to *lectio divina*. Have you participated in a small group that used this approach to praying scripture? Using the same questions listed in the meditation, read Isaiah 2:1-5. See if you sense a a nudge from God for you.

Second Week of Advent

O Wisdom, who came forth from the mouth of the
Most High, reaching from end to end, and ordering all
things mightily and sweetly: Come, and teach us the
way of prudence.

When I was an adolescent, my maternal grandfather would
say to me, "Hovaness, you're smart, but you are not wise.
Smart is not enough." I'm sure that he tired of seeing my eyes
roll in response to his observation. Now I wish that I had asked
Pop Kamajian to explain his statement so that I could have
savored his perspective.

How do you understand wisdom? The antiphon speaks in a
straightforward manner. When I think of wisdom and the Bible,
two passages of scripture jump from memory. The first passage
is Proverbs 1:2, which explains the purpose of the proverbs and
reads as follows: "For learning about wisdom and instruction,
for understanding words of insight."

Before I write about that verse's significance, I want to
explain some personal and Armenian history. The missionary
Saint Gregory the Illuminator brought healing to Drtad (also
known as Tiridates III or Tiridates the Great), the pagan king of
Armenia, and the king became a Christian. He then declared in

royal fashion that if Christianity served him well, Christianity would be good for all the Armenian people. Missionaries and priests received freedom to go among the pagan people and convert them to Christianity. Armenia declared itself a Christian nation in the year 301.

Christianity grew among the people, but one obstacle stood in the way of that growth. These religious leaders preached and taught from the Greek and Syrian versions of scripture. They did not use the vernacular language for the simple reason that Armenia did not yet have a written alphabet.

How could there not be an alphabet? The first Armenians settled in the mountainous area surrounding Mount Ararat around the year 3500 BCE. Archaeologists have discovered in the caves winepresses, shoes, and other items that date back to approximately 3000. In my personal collection, I have a potsherd dated to approximately 3500 BCE, a non-museum quality item given by an archaeologist to my cousin on a visit to Armenia. The Armenian people are an old culture, surviving among the mountains of Asia Minor.

The Armenian language was, like all languages of that era, a means of oral communication. Because of the people's simple needs, no one had developed an Armenian alphabet—and that lack hindered the church's growth. A priest named Mesrob Mashtots (in the Eastern Armenian language his first name is Mesrop) worked to invent a written alphabet, completing his task around the year 405. Development of the Armenian alphabet led to the next facet of Mesrob's work: the translation of the Bible into Armenian. The first sentence translated by Mesrob into Armenian was Proverbs 1:2, which, translated from the Armenian, reads, "To know wisdom and instruction; to perceive the words of understanding."

The wisdom that followed the work of translation brought the light of Christ to the people. Christianity became a life-giving force among the people. Commitments to Christ remained strong over the centuries despite hardship and persecution. To know wisdom and to perceive the words of understanding is the purpose behind the writing and the study of many books. From a faith perspective, reading the Bible opens us to the wisdom and love of God and to the holy presence itself.

In this season of Advent, we gain wisdom as we wait and come to new understandings of timing and patience. John 1:14 implies this sense of God's patience: "The Word became flesh and lived among us." When I read this passage, my imagination inserts the phrase "at the right time" so that the verse reads "At the right time the Word became flesh." Maybe Israel had grown and matured enough at that point. Maybe the weighty needs of the world required divine intervention.

Job 28 also comes to mind when I think of wisdom. The chapter offers a break as Job attempts to defend himself and God against the arguments of his friends. Job 28 speaks of mines for precious metals and gems, then asks, "But where shall wisdom be found?" (v. 12). Like Proverbs 1:2, the answer in Job points toward our response to God: "Truly, the fear of the Lord, that is wisdom." Eugene Peterson translates the answer to the question in the following way: "Then he addressed the human race: 'Here it is! Fear-of-the-Lord—that's Wisdom, and Insight means shunning evil'" (Job 28:28, THE MESSAGE).

As we move toward Christmas, may we see beyond the surface and perceive God at work in the world, transforming every person through love.

20—Seeing the Last

Take time now to read Micah 5:2-5a. As you read the passage, what portions stick with you?

Throughout scripture, the books of the Bible proclaim principles of God's justice. Perhaps the basic principle concerns the economy of God's reign. Jesus said, "Many who are first will be last, and the last will be first" (Matt. 19:30) and again, "So the last will be first, and the first will be last" (Matt. 20:16).

Centuries before Matthew recorded Jesus' words, the prophet Micah speaks to the people for God. In that time, as in our time, people ranked cities and tribes in a hierarchy of importance. Jerusalem rates ahead of all other towns and villages in Israel in the same way that New York today ranks considerably ahead of my hometown of Hopewell, Virginia. Bethlehem may have ranked on the same level as Hopewell or Hoboken in the popular mind. Micah runs against the flow of that culture when in verse 2 the oracle reads, "But you, O Bethlehem . . . who are one of the little clans of Judah, / from you shall come forth for me one who is to rule in Israel."

Micah prophesied in the eighth century BCE, and I feel reasonably certain that people did not take Micah's prophecy seriously. Jesus said, "Prophets are not without honor, except in their hometown, and among their own kin, and in their own house" (Mark 6:4). People accept the words of prophets only in retrospect. Scripture shows us prophets, such as Elijah, fleeing for their lives, while the people admire false prophets. A crowd wants to throw Jesus off a cliff. (See Luke 4:16-30.) We see the rejection of prophets in our own time.

In the twentieth century many people rejected Dorothy Day and Martin Luther King Jr. during their lifetimes. As in biblical times, people flocked after more popular speakers who proclaimed that they were God's true representatives. After the deaths of Day and King, a veneer of respectability attached to them. While the self-proclaimed prophets are largely forgotten, many people who once distanced themselves from Day and King now quote the two. So who are God's prophets today?

Who self-proclaims as a prophet? What will we think of these people in twenty years? What will history say?

Still we consider Micah's prophecy. In biblical times, people probably reacted, *From Bethlehem shall come a ruler? That is not possible.* We have the luxury of looking back at both Micah and Jesus and then affirming that Jesus of Nazareth came from Bethlehem of the house and lineage of the great King David. Even as we affirm this sacred history, we know that Micah's prophecy is accurate. The last will be first; lowly Bethlehem will be elevated.

How can we begin to see people in the same way that God sees people? How shall we move forward in this time of Advent-Christmas-Epiphany to bear witness to God's love?

Many conversations today brand people as winners or losers. Winners are wonderful; losers are not. In the time of Micah, people may have branded Bethlehem as a loser. Branding or labeling people comes easily. When we label individuals, our vision does not penetrate the surface. We demonstrate a smartness that lacks wisdom. When we label people, I believe that we fail to demonstrate Jesus' love for the whole world. Remembering that the last will be first gives us reason enough to stop our labeling and to see each person as a gift created by God. The challenge of Christian discipleship comes in seeing Christ within each person—whether or not that person understands the love of Christ as we do. This method of seeing the Christ in each person is our first act of discernment, of a seeing with the eyes of the heart rather than viewing outward characteristics alone. Who will you see today? I hope that you see and meet Christ throughout the day. As you see Christ today, see him as the one prophesied by Micah: as one who shall rule in Israel and as one whose life and teachings govern us.

Notice that the passage ends "and he shall be the one of peace" (v. 5). Become open to experience the peace of Christ, to live with this peace, and to extend the peace of Christ to all you encounter. This message comes not only from Micah but from the angels who announce the birth of Jesus to shepherds in a field. We offer the message of peace throughout these holy days.

> **God, we give thanks for your love and offer praise for the gifts of life. Through your love, prepare us for this celebration. Help us experience the blessed gift of Incarnation and the way you shared your life of peace with us through Jesus. Guide us to demonstrate your love in all that we do today. Marked by the love of Jesus, we pray. Amen.**

19 — An Editor

The newspaper editor James Montgomery also wrote poetry. Born in 1771, Montgomery died in 1854. We may recognize his name as a hymn writer. Authorities jailed Montgomery for his crusading work to abolish slavery and to end the exploitation of children as chimney sweeps. (For more about chimney sweeps, see my book *A World Worth Saving*). Montgomery composed several hundred hymns, including "Angels from the Realms of Glory," "Go to Dark Gethsemane," "Prayer Is the Soul's Sincere Desire," and "Stand Up and Bless the Lord."

Montgomery also wrote "Hail to the Lord's Anointed," a hymn inspired by Psalm 72. We usually sing the hymn during the season of Advent. Montgomery looks back from our post-Easter vantage point to name the promises that surround Christ's coming. I ask you to reflect on his words today.

> Hail to the Lord's Anointed, great David's greater Son!
> Hail in the time appointed, his reign on earth begun!
> He comes to break oppression, to set the captive free;
> to take away transgression, and rule in equity.

Notice the work Montgomery attributes to the Messiah, the Christ. The hymn reminds us that God offers preferential action to the poor and oppressed. Throughout the Bible, especially when we see the Hebrew people in captivity in Egypt, God breaks oppressive rule. God offers a freedom that goes far beyond the oppression of physical boundaries. God's freedom includes mental and emotional freedom. Most significant within the act of breaking oppression is God's gift of forgiveness and removing the guilt-laden burden of our transgressions.

He comes with succor speedy to those who suffer wrong;
to help the poor and needy, and bid the weak be strong;
to give them songs for sighing, their darkness turn to light,
whose souls, condemned and dying, are precious in his sight.

Montgomery's hymn reminds us that God aids those who experience the wrongs of life, who live in oppressive conditions and receive oppressive labels from others. How does this affect our response when we hear disparaging remarks about ghettos or refugees? Pay attention to the ways in which friends and leaders discuss people. Every resident in each ghetto and every refugee bears the image of Christ. Christ values and holds each one dear, "condemned and dying." I pray that we may all remember these words and hold in love these people beloved by Christ.

Montgomery notes that God gives songs amid struggle. "Hail to the Lord's Anointed" offers words of hope. "We Shall Overcome," "Venceremos," "Hymn to Freedom," "The Times They Are a'Changin'," and "Mer Hayastan" ("Our Armenia"— sung when the Armenian nation was a memory) are some of the many songs that energized liberation movements. Despite the wearying effect of oppression, these songs held dreams and hopes before the people. I imagine that the people leaving Egypt under Moses' leadership sang many songs of hope and trust in God.

He shall come down like showers upon the fruitful earth;
love, joy, and hope, like flowers, spring in his path to birth.
Before him, on the mountains, shall peace, the herald, go,
and righteousness, in fountains, from hill to valley flow.

Montgomery names five attributes of Christ: love, joy, hope, peace, and righteousness. Montgomery's reference to peace and righteousness remind me of Psalm 85:10: "Steadfast love and faithfulness will meet; righteousness and peace will kiss each other." Eugene Peterson's translation may offer greater clarity: "Love and Truth meet in the street, Right Living and Whole Living embrace and kiss! Truth sprouts green from the ground, Right Living pours down from the skies!" (THE MESSAGE). Take time today to consider the peace and righteousness of Christ.

To him shall prayer unceasing and daily vows ascend;
his kingdom still increasing, a kingdom without end.
The tide of time shall never his covenant remove;
his name shall stand forever; that name to us is love.

Montgomery's text echoes the message that resounds across the Bible. The reign of God grows, as a mustard plant, in forms uncontrolled, wild, and beautiful. This reign continues until the end of the age and beyond whatever that end may be. Montgomery's final line focuses us again on the Incarnation and summarizes the whole of the hymn: "That name to us is love." Nothing other than the love of Christ will liberate the oppressed, heal the sick and dying, and bring justice and righteousness and peace to the people of the world. That love remains the heart of our Advent-Christmas-Epiphany proclamation.

Great God, the cloud of witnesses stretches from the Bible to our time and beyond. While some witnesses are famous, others are little known. We give thanks for the faith and witness of James Montgomery. May we

continue to receive guidance from the past for this day
and for our future life. Amen.

18 — Prudence

The Wisdom antiphon ends with a curious word—*prudence.*
We commonly understand prudence as cautiousness and the
avoidance of risk. We may know "Dear Prudence," a song written by John Lennon and included on the 1968 Beatles' recording known by its solid white cover. We may associate the word
with the theory of law known as jurisprudence. We may know
someone with the relatively rare name Prudence. For some out-
landish reason of faulty memory, I associate prudence with the
name of a dour character in a novel set in Puritan New England.
We do not typically use the word, but here prudence is the final
word in a prayer concerning God's wisdom in Christ.

Do we believe that the antiphon asks the Divine to teach
us to avoid risk? That may be a valid interpretation given the
ways we understand prudence today; however, that meaning
seems doubtful. After all, God risked revelation with Moses on
Mount Sinai. Before that encounter, God risked love in free-
ing the Hebrew people from captivity in Egypt. God-with-us in
the birth of a helpless baby is definitely not an act of prudence.
Becoming human as an infant is not the way of prudence as we
generally understand that word. Jesus does not demonstrate the
cautious understanding of prudence when, as a mature adult, he
challenges the religious and cultural authorities.

Speaking of Jesus' birth requires our awareness that proclamation may sometimes camouflage the tremendous risk God
took in becoming human.

I invite you to a quick journey into the roots of this word
prudence. The pre-Christian Greek philosopher Aristotle (c. 422
BCE) identified four cardinal virtues that gave people moral value.

These qualities Aristotle named prudence, temperance, courage, and justice. He thought that these qualities helped people to live with integrity and clarity while doing what is right. Aristotle thought that prudence formed the basis for temperance, courage, and justice. Many centuries later the Christian theologian Thomas Aquinas (1225–74) developed a broader moral understanding by adding faith, hope, and charity to Aristotle's four virtues. Aquinas, like Aristotle, thought that the most important of the virtues was prudence. Every other moral response developed from the virtue known as prudence.

So what is prudence, and why does the antiphon beseech God to teach us the way of prudence? The word comes from the Latin word *prudentia*, which means "foresight and wisdom." Prudence combines knowledge with perception to discern right and wrong action. The quality of prudence helps us distinguish when an action is cowardly or reckless and when an action is courageous.

O Wisdom, come, and teach us the way of prudence. Asking for prudence is the same as praying for wisdom and discernment.

Today many voices clamor for our attention. Businesses tug at us, especially in the pre-Christmas season, trying to convince us to buy glittering items that we probably would never pick up without the heavy commercial appeals. The e-mails and packets sent by charities show us many heart-rending photos of overwhelming need around the world. Politicians offer a wide range of solutions to national and international matters. Financial institutions offer their versions of economic salvation. Churches differ in their understanding of the gospel and its impact on the daily life of the world. How do we decide what to do? Which charity should we support? How shall we spend our money? Without the prudence or discernment that comes from God, we will become frozen by choice.

What does prudence—this way of discernment—suggest that we do in response to the noise of the free market? We look with open minds. We apply our intelligence first to determine our choices. We use our memory to determine whether we or someone else has made a similar decision. If so, we ask or remember what happened. We seek a sense of foresight to understand potential consequences of our action. We seek the wisdom of faith, the vision of hope, and the action of love to inform our decision. Having used these gifts, we decide. We choose. We act. Our actions begin in prudence—wisdom and discernment.

This way of prudence also reflects what Albert Outler described as "the Wesleyan quadrilateral." In brief, Outler said that theological reflection relied on four sources: scripture, reason, tradition, and experience. To Outler, the Bible is the primary source for reflection. Reason, tradition, and experience are crucial aspects that create a vibrant perspective on faith.

Prudence may not be a word that jumps out at anyone during this season and yet, prudence offers us a way forward as we follow Christ.

Loving God, open us to your Holy Spirit and form us in the way of Christ. Help us to live with wisdom and discernment so that we may sense your movement in our lives and throughout the earth. Amen.

17 – Dreams

Have you noticed the number of significant dreams in the Bible? While it may not be the first dream recorded, many people know the story of Jacob's dream as he slept at Bethel. Angels descended and ascended on a ladder that reached to heaven. (Read Genesis 28:10-22.) Another well-known dream came to Peter, who dreamed of a sheet lowered from the heavens. On the sheet were clean and unclean animals. A voice told Peter to eat, and Peter refused, saying that he had never touched unclean food. Three times the voice replied, "What God has made clean, you must not profane" (Acts 10:9-16).

Closer to us in this season are the dreams that surround Jesus' birth. When Joseph learns of his betrothed's pregnancy, he decides to divorce her. In a dream, an angel tells Joseph to stay with Mary because the son conceived in her will save the people from their sins. (See Matthew 1:18-23.) The magi receive a warning in a dream to return home and avoid Herod. (See Matthew 2:12.) In another dream, an angel warns Joseph to escape to Egypt. (See Matthew 2:13.) Later still, an angel appears in a dream and tells Joseph to return with his family to Israel. (Read Matthew 2:19-23.)

Do you pay attention to your dreams, or does your mind erase those dreams before you become aware of them? The Episcopal priest John Sanford helps people understand that the God who spoke through dreams to people in biblical times continues to speak in the same way today.

In *Dreams: God's Forgotten Language*, Sanford wrote that he had been studying dream analysis when

> I was struck by the fact that the Bible also believed in the analysis of dreams. The point of view of the Bible was that God spoke through dreams. My experience corroborated this viewpoint, because I could see in my dreams a spirit at work that seemed to have a goal in mind that transcended my ego and its meager bit of consciousness. (ix)

I believe Sanford's wisdom about dreams offers us guidance for prayer. I know that I have pondered a number of dreams over the years and have gained insight from that reflection.

I do not intend to teach dream interpretation but to encourage us to pay attention to our dreams and then pray about them. Our prayers begin in listening to our dreams. The God who spoke to Jacob, Joseph, and the magi speaks still to us. We may need to spend time pursuing personal meaning beneath the surface events of our dreams. Many of the characters in a dream represent aspects of our own personalities, including aspects that we prefer to hide. The actions and symbols in our dreams often point to a larger issue.

Part One of Sanford's *Dreams* offers examples of dreams that intersect waking life and call for spiritual response. We may discover in our dreams a need to heal a broken relationship or a call to release something that binds us. We may hear God's invitation to show love to a stranger or to follow Jesus in a new way. Listening to our dreams can guide us to spiritual insight.

As we work on our dreams and pray, we engage in a dialogue. God invites, and we respond. We speak of our own hopes and desires. We pray for healing for friends and perhaps for ourselves. We may pray for healing for one we do not know but were asked to pray for that person's needs. As in every conversation, we use words and silence to communicate.

I suggest that you pray in more expansive ways. Our prayers will seek wisdom and understanding. Our prayers for healing will include intercession for the community, the state, the nation, and the world. Trust that God is responding to your prayers. Listen for God in the promptings of thoughts and dreams, of friends and strangers, in reading the Bible and other resources.

God answers. The answers may not be the desired response, but the answer is always formed in love and reflects God's love for us. We understand that God loves in deeper ways than any other love we know on earth. That love seeks goodness for us and for others. As many people throughout history have thought and said, "I have lived long enough to be thankful that God answered some of my prayers in the negative. No matter the response, I will love because that is the way Christ taught."

God, am I quiet enough to hear your invitation in my dreams? Am I picking up your signals in dreams and in relationships? What would you like me to do today as I follow the teachings of Jesus? Amen.

Questions for the Week

- What distinction do you make between being smart and being wise?
- In everyday life we tend to think of the first—in a category or a race or an election or in grades—as superior. The Bible offers a different wisdom. What does it mean for everyday life if we treat the last as first?
- What did you learn from the meditation concerning prudence?
- How do the songs of Christmas speak to your spirituality? When do you take time to reflect on the words of these songs?
- What kinds of dreams do you have? In what ways do you sense God speaking to you through your dreams?

Third Week of Advent

O Root of Jesse, who stands for an ensign of the people, before whom kings shall keep silence and to whom the Gentiles shall make their supplication: Come, and deliver us and tarry not.

I live in an area in which the colleges with Tiger, Gamecock, and Bulldog mascots have many traditions, and the colleges instill those traditions in all new students. They teach songs with hand gestures and they teach the local lore, remembering athletic contests, fabled students, and more. Every college does this. In 1940 my father went to college one trimester. Several times he told me about an elderly professor who despised students because sophomores painted white stripes on his pet black mule, causing the death of the mule. He reasoned that first-year students would become sophomores and juniors had been sophomores and therefore, the hatred was deserved. Years after my father's death, I talked with a church member who attended that college in the post-World War II years. I said something vague about my father's professor who despised students, and the church member immediately said, "Oh, you mean Professor Borkey. He was retired when I was there, but I heard about him and his mule." Tradition and lore travel well.

Governments have their own traditions. We witness the pomp of royal coronations. We see layers of tradition, for example, in the president's state of the union address. That tradition actually begins with a formal invitation from the Speaker of the House to the president to address a joint session of the US Senate and House of Representatives. After the members of congress and guests have assembled, the Deputy Sergeant of Arms announces in loud voice the vice president, who is escorted to his or her seat. Next the Sergeant at Arms announces the chief justice and other members of the Supreme Court. Eventually select members of Congress escort the president to the dais for the speech. So goes the protocol, a portion of tradition in the US government.

The church probably leads all institutions in its traditions. We invoke traditions when we baptize or marry within a church. Our sense of tradition informs our understanding of the Lord's Supper—and our *particular* tradition shapes the name we call that sacrament: Holy Communion, the Mass, the Eucharist, the memorial meal. We nod toward our traditions when acolytes light candles. We have layers of tradition concerning clergy.

I invite you to consider the importance of tradition, which is not something we keep simply because it is old. Custom better describes those activities we do simply because they are old. Tradition gives life, especially as we focus on the meaning and purpose underlying our practice, while custom involves doing something solely because "we've always done it." Every tradition began as something new, and that innovative activity—when first practiced—brought meaning and value to an individual. Soon enough, the individual's innovative effort led to a community practice of the original act because the community began to see value in the practice. We witness and participate in the birth of a tradition.

One post-World War II innovation grew into a tradition known as the chrismon tree. A member of Ascension Lutheran Church in Danville, Virginia, in 1957 suggested decorating the sanctuary Christmas tree with symbols and monograms of Jesus Christ. In the mid-1950s, this idea seemed novel and never done before, but soon more churches understood that the practice gave a new meaning to the Advent-Christmas period, birthing the chrismon tree tradition. Larger numbers of churches adopted this new tradition so that denominations began offering congregations guidance for liturgies and teaching points. Today while many churches decorate their sanctuaries with chrismon trees, some members have no idea how this tradition began.

Notice how this antiphon indicates the ancestry and tradition of the Christ. Tradition nurtures us, giving us roots and a desire to grow and to add to that tradition. What traditions during Advent-Christmas-Epiphany nurture you? Why do you continue to keep these traditions? Have you developed new traditions of devotion or ministry?

This book, I believe, continues in a line of tradition as it reflects on some ancient prayers, and I hope that my reflection will add something new to our common understanding of these prayers in this season of life. As you read this week's meditations and prayers, may you experience wonder and awe.

16 — Roots

Many of my friends spend time doing genealogical research. They go through historic records to discover their family roots. An uncle of mine traced his maternal genealogy to about 1860, but he confirmed how sparse were the records and documentation of Armenians prior to the 1915 genocide. My paternal genealogy begins with the arrival of my grandparents in the

United States in the early twentieth century. In fact, some years after my grandfather's arrival, he received a green card that stated that he arrived here on the "SS Unknown." While I have visited the Republic of Armenia, I cannot visit the area that my paternal grandparents left. I know only that they escaped from a village in what is now eastern Turkey. Despite the lack of specific knowledge, the roots go far; they go deep for every one of us.

We know, in part thanks to the work of Alex Haley and his book *Roots*, that the word *roots* refers to a descendant or a branch of a family. Our religion proclaims that our roots go beyond our biological families. We dare to claim kinship with Jesus and his ancestors in faith.

The prophet Isaiah addresses the critical nature of such faithful roots: "A shoot shall come out from the stump of Jesse, and a branch shall grow out of his roots" (Isa. 11:1). We read about a dead tree's remains; yet, something living comes from the dead stump. Isaiah's hope-filled words reflect an awareness of history as a basis for current reality. As one who spoke for God, Isaiah offered a vision of the holy future toward which we move.

Isaiah prophesied in the eighth century BCE. Jump eight centuries from Isaiah to the Gospel of Matthew. Chapter 1 provides an account of Jesus' genealogy, which fills in the ancestral gaps. We can easily skip over this section of Matthew to get to the parts that are more interesting and inviting, but then we miss the significance of the genealogy that Matthew presents. (Perhaps this section of Matthew supplies the best argument for reading and studying the fullness of the Bible, not simply the New Testament.) In Matthew's genealogy of Jesus, we learn about Obed, Jesse, David, and others in this holy history. Obed, the father of Jesse, was the son of Ruth. Ruth was a Moabite woman who married Mahlon, son of Elimelech and Naomi. Elimelech and Naomi were Jews who traveled to Moab because of a famine in Judah. These migrants sought to survive in an alien land. Their son married a non-Jew, a Moabite outside the culture of Judah and Israel, breaking a cultural taboo about preservation of the ethnic group. Beyond preserving the tribe, why is this information of value to us? Even the genealogy of Jesus points to a godly embrace and love for all people. God's love breaks through taboos of borders and demarcations.

As I look back at Isaiah's prophecy and Matthew's genealogy, I also recall a portion of a prayer from Dag Hammarskjöld: "For all that has been—Thanks!" (*Markings*, 89) I pray these words every morning. Most of the time I relate those words to the events of the previous day—sometimes the week before. My devotional time often feels focused on my experience, on the me-myself-mine of life; yet, Hammarskjold's prayer never seems limited to the self. If I take seriously the meaning of "For all that has been," then I realize that I am praying about the history that I share with you and with Jesus and with the others who have gone before me. Suddenly Hammarskjold's words begin to focus on roots from a new angle. Now I begin to pray with a sense of gratitude for what God has done throughout history, the history I know and the history I do not know. The prayer connects me with all the years in which God has been transforming the world. My prayers now expand to embrace time and place, the earth and all that has been.

"For all that has been—Thanks!" Those six words from Dag Hammarskjöld's journal expand the borders of my prayer life. In what ways are the borders of your prayer life expanding?

God, you have given us roots. Show us that our lives build upon the past, that the past remains a gift for this time, a heritage of blessing. Encourage us to live so that future generations will build upon what we have done and will offer their own gratitude for the life we share. Amen.

15 — Decorated Trees

One friend decorates her Christmas tree with solid white lights and religious ornaments. Another decorates the tree with ornaments that feature Elvis Presley and a variety of bright flashing and chasing lights. Still other friends mix religious and secular ornaments on their trees and throughout their living spaces. If you put up a Christmas tree, when do you put it on display? When you take the tree down may determine when you put the tree up. If you keep the tree up through the twelve days of Christmas, then you probably put up the tree in the middle of December.

The Christmas tree is a curious tradition. One legend of Christmas tells us that Martin Luther decorated the first Christmas tree with light, placing candles on an evergreen and saying that they shined like the stars. As much as I appreciate Luther, no historical evidence supports this rather dangerous idea of Luther's lighting candles on a tree.

Long before Luther, non-Christian religions revered trees in different ways. Romans decorated their homes with evergreens during the Saturnalia festival, and Druids decorated oak trees with apples. In the late Middle Ages, plays celebrating the Nativity were performed outdoors. As part of the Christmas celebration, these plays connected the nativity of Christ with the fall from paradise. Paradise trees, hung with fruit, were part of the décor. When those attending the plays became so rowdy that authorities banned them, people continued the custom of the "paradise tree" in their homes. Instead of placing fruit on the trees, they decorated the trees with cookies baked to look like Communion wafers. From those round cookies developed the round ornaments we use today.

When Ascension Lutheran Church in Danville, Virginia, adapted the suggestion to decorate the sanctuary Christmas tree with chrismon symbols and monograms of Jesus Christ—soon many congregations began to decorate their trees with these symbols of Christ made from cloth or plastic or Styrofoam. For many people, the chrismons—a combination of Christ and monogram—became an introduction to traditional symbols such as the Chi Rho or the Alpha and Omega. Different cross designs may decorate a tree, and each cross has its particular history. Palm branches remind us of how the crowds waved branches when Jesus entered Jerusalem. (See Matthew 21:1-11.) A descending dove may point to the Holy Spirit, and a butterfly can suggest the Resurrection. The lamb reminds us of Christ the unblemished lamb, or it may remind us of Jesus' instruction to Peter: "Feed my lambs" (John 21:15). Other symbols stand for the Trinity or the miracles Jesus did. A globe may evoke the thought that God has "the whole world in his hands" or that the meek shall inherit the earth. Wheat and grapes may point us toward the beatitude that "those who hunger and thirst for righteousness, for they shall be satisfied" (Matt. 5:6, NASB).

Unpacking the meaning of our Christmas decorations is a fun way to explore Christian faith and discipleship. If you have children in your home or if you are in ministry with children, take time to talk about the meanings of the many symbols of this season.

Christmas trees and chrismons serve as pointers to a deeper reality of the season. In the best of ways, they invite us to see with the eyes of the heart and to become more like Christ, showing love in all encounters. During this season, live with a sense of grace and love as you deal with people becoming overly stressed by advertising, finances, family, work or lack of work, and more. Do not, for example, become offended by a store clerk who wished you a "happy holiday." Maybe management insisted that everyone say those words at the checkout counter. A sarcastic or angry response in such situations does not give a very positive witness to the love of God for all people. This season becomes a time to let go of our rights and to let God work through us and through others for the transformation of the world.

From all the Christmas trees, with both sacred and secular decorations, see the words of Jesus: "Let your light shine before others, so that they may see your good works and give glory to your Father in heaven" (Matt. 5:16).

> **God, will you decorate our lives the way the chrismon trees are decorated? As we see decorated trees, may they remind us of your love for the earth and all who live upon it. Help us to see the wonder of each decoration, an example of creativity and creation. Keep us from becoming jaded or cynical; allow us to see with newness of faith the transformation you are working throughout the world. Amen.**

14—Saint Nicholas

The Santa Claus tradition has roots that stretch back to Bishop Nicholas of the ancient Greek town of Myra. Bishop Nicholas died on December 6, 343, and many celebrate his life on this day. An uncle, who was a bishop, raised the orphan Nicholas and later ordained Nicholas as a priest. The Roman emperor Diocletian imprisoned Nicholas during the persecution of Christians in the early fourth century. Diocletian regarded all Christians as enemies of the state. But Nicholas persevered in his faith. Constantine freed him from prison when he became emperor. Years later Nicholas attended the Council of Nicaea (325 CE) and served as a witness who shaped the church. This first ecumenical council came together to seek consensus on a variety of issues, especially the divine-human nature of Christ.

The council worked hard on this matter, created a large portion of the Nicene Creed, and settled on a uniform dating of Easter.

People referred to Nicholas as the Wonderworker because of miracles attributed to him. Whether or not those miracles happened, we know Nicholas as one who secretly aided those in need. Many legends surround his secret giving. Perhaps the story most well known concerns a poor father whose three daughters needed marriage dowries. According to legend, Nicholas placed three bags of gold in the house while the family slept. One later variation of this story shows the saint putting the gold bags in stockings that hung to dry. Still another variation tells that Nicholas tossed the bags of gold through the house chimney. From the very real bishop of history developed our traditions surrounding Santa Claus, a name that comes to us through the Dutch wording for Saint Nicholas—Sinterklass.

The life of Nicholas provides a model for Christian discipleship. His prayerful devotion to God led to acts of mercy and piety. Nicholas practiced the basic disciplines of Christian devotion: Bible reading, prayer, public worship, frequency in receiving Holy Communion, fasting, and living within a community of faith. Personal prayer and reading scripture surely focused Nicholas on the work at hand. Such prayer led to his openness to the nudges of the Holy Spirit, nudges that led to his giving alms to the needy. The same practices of personal prayer and daily Bible reading, public worship, frequent Communion, fasting, and community life shape our lives today. These practices cultivate a deeper faith for our daily living. As these practices work within us, we will also do deeds of kindness and mercy to all.

What do I mean by deeds of kindness and mercy? Saint Nicholas offers an answer: seeing a need and addressing it. In Matthew 25:31-46, Jesus gives us specific direction. He speaks of feeding the hungry, giving water to the thirsty, welcoming strangers, clothing the naked, visiting the sick and those in prison.

The love of Christ motivates us to act. Being cynical about the motives of the person holding the "homeless and hungry" sign and asking for donations is easy. Being cynical about those who come to the food pantry comes much too naturally, especially when social media shape our thinking through unsubstantiated stories and the manufacturing of rumors. Our cynicism allows us to shield our hearts and our consciences. Love breaks down the hardness surrounding our hearts. We give because God gives to us. We love because God loves us. That sounds simple, and I intend it to be uncomplicated. I think of words in the New Testament: "Be kind to one another, tenderhearted, forgiving one another, as God in Christ has forgiven you" (Eph. 4:32). We visit those in need, give aid, offer what we have because Saint Nicholas did that and because Jesus said to do it.

I encourage you to read the whole Bible and let it slowly nurture you in faith. One caution about Bible reading: Some of my friends participate in "read the Bible in a year" programs. I am glad that they are reading the Bible because it remains the foundation of faith. Even so, I invite and encourage them and you to read the Bible slowly. Avoid speed-reading the Bible; rather, ponder the layers of meaning throughout scripture. Please don't rush any facets of our Christian spiritual practice.

> **God of the ages, Saint Nicholas persevered through imprisonment for his faith. He did not become cynical, but showed love. What will you show us to keep us from becoming cynical? Bring health and healing to our lives so that we may witness for you through our acts of generosity, compassion, and love. Amen.**

13 — Decking

I confess that no matter the season of the year, I hum the opening measures of "Deck the Halls." I hum only the first measures of that song, creating a musical scale that descends and ascends. I do not know when or why I began this habit. Musicologists identify "Deck the Halls" as a medieval Welsh melody, originally used for dance. Most of us identify this song with Christmas or the New Year celebration.

Consider the words of these two verses—minus most of the Fa la las. (As with all folk songs, the wording may vary from that familiar to you):

Deck the halls with boughs of holly,
'Tis the season to be jolly,
Don we now our gay apparel,
Troll the ancient Christmas carol.

See the blazing Yule before us,
Strike the harp and join the chorus.
Follow me in merry measure,
While I tell of Yuletide treasure,
Fa la la la la la la la la.

I know these words have little to do with Jesus' birth. Those who approach Christmas from a strictly religious perspective may dismiss this song. I'd like us to consider how "Deck the Halls" reflects our own practices. We decorate our homes and living spaces for Christmas. We decorate with evergreen trees and holly and strive to make our houses festive. We wear festive clothing, including red plaids and sweaters with various scenes or symbols of Christmas. We sing together as choruses. We strive for gaiety, laughter, and joy as we embrace a variety of Christmas traditions.

These are the outward signs of our joy. But what of our inner decoration? How are we preparing ourselves to celebrate the birth of Jesus the Christ? What are we doing to clean out the old baggage and make room for the fresh love of Christ? I could suggest that we read the Bible and pray, but that is the answer always given. Many of us do just that and still feel weighed down by that old baggage. We may simply shrug when others greet us with holiday joy and respond, "Everything's OK—same old same old." Yet, within us a soul cries out to be born in a new and more vital way.

Try this spiritual experiment: Instead of using your eyes to see the world, enlarge your heart and allow it to guide you. Let your heart overrule your head whenever you feel tempted to react or respond with cynicism.

What if you were to adopt the words of "Deck the Halls" as your prayer for the season? What might happen if you invite God to deck your symbolic inner hallways with the evergreen spirit? The various evergreen trees and shrubs represent anticipation, hope, immortality, and eternity. If God so clothes us in those new garments, we will interact in new ways with the world. And what could we experience if the Yuletide or the Christmas treasure grew more profoundly within us? We would behave kindly to the grouch next door. We would give generously and surprisingly to the one asking for alms. Our loving response to the demanding one may shock that person into a recognition of his or her ill-mannered ways, leading to another transformation.

Over and over we hear that Advent prepares us to celebrate the love of God in Jesus Christ. The celebration never involves the lavish nature of our outer decorations but our inner selves and how we show the love of Christ to all people.

The early Christians fasted during Advent to prepare spiritually for Christmas. By the fifth century, people may have missed the spiritual significance of such fasting and prayer. Pope Leo the Great (Leo I), whose papacy lasted more than twenty years, addressed Advent's outer/inner preparation around the year 450. Pope Leo spoke about fasting:

> Since fasting is not the only means to secure health for our souls, let us adorn our fasting with works of mercy. . . . Our fast must be turned into a banquet for the poor. Let us devote time and effort to the underprivileged, the widow and the orphan; let us show sympathy to the afflicted and reconcile the estranged; provide lodging for the wanderer and relieve the oppressed; give clothing to the naked and cherish the sick.

I realize the words of Pope Leo seem far removed from the words of "Deck the Halls," but these words offer direction as we do deeds of generosity, kindness, and love.

Today use the words of "Deck the Halls" as a prayer. Or write a prayer based on themes you see in the carol. Here, for example, is one prayer:

> **God, decorate my inner self with the evergreen spirit of Christ. Renew hope in me so that I may not fall prey to the cynical spirit of this age; rather, help me sense your grace in all that happens. Decorate my inner self so that my outer being shows your love. Amen.**

Or

> **Lord God, let your Spirit blaze before me, behind me, within me. Let your love burn away and consume all that detracts from Christ in me. Amen.**

Now it's your turn.

Questions for the Week

- What traditions are important to your family and to your church? What makes these practices significant?
- What Christmas traditions seem dated and meaningless to you?
- When do you find it easy to give to others? When is it difficult?
- What marks of Christian discipleship seem visible in Saint Nicholas? What spiritual disciplines do you imagine that he would have practiced?
- What practices can you release to create more space for acts of service and generosity toward others? What new practices of generosity can you add?
- Does your church have a chrismon tree or an Advent wreath? How would you react if your church stopped using these symbols? How would that change your understanding of Advent-Christmas?

Fourth Week of Advent

O Key of David and Scepter of the house of Israel, who opens and no one shuts, who shuts and no one opens: Come, and bring forth from prison the captive who sits in darkness and in the shadow of death.

I once lived in a farmhouse that sat on multiple acres with apple trees, a Methodist church parsonage with two doors. The front door of the house could not be locked, and the back door could not be unlocked. So much for keys in that locale! Keys are necessary to lock our cars, homes, property, and places of work. We sometimes lose keys. We now feel secure with digital locks for our cars and homes and other belongings, including our computers and various social network accounts—until a hacker comes along or we forget the password.

The key of life is another matter altogether. As we celebrate the incarnation of God in Jesus, we begin to see through the external aspects of the Christmas holy days to the inner meaning and purpose of this time. We pray the antiphon.

The key of life, the one who opens and no one shuts, the one who shuts and no one opens—is this not the Christ and Christ alone? This is our Christmas proclamation, our announcement of good news to a world in great need. Jesus is the key of life, the one of whom angels sang, the one who causes our lives to move in a way far removed from a life without Christ. Our understanding of the antiphon hinges on how we think about the final clause: "bring forth from prison the captive who sits in darkness and in the shadow of death." This antiphon seems based on Isaiah's prophecies of the Messiah as suffering servant, particularly Isaiah 42:6-7 and Isaiah 49:8-13.

To understand Isaiah 42:1-9 more fully, we go back to the context. Despite the annual Passover remembrance, the people of Israel wandered away from the covenant made with God. Over and over in their history, we see Israel go astray and then discover anew the covenantal relationship with God. In the sixth century BCE, however, the unimaginable happened. Babylon invaded Israel and destroyed the Temple. The Babylonians plundered the land and took the Jewish people into bondage. From this Babylonian captivity came Psalm 137 and the haunting words, "By the rivers of Babylon—there we sat down and there we wept when we remembered Zion" (v. 1). To these captive people, Isaiah speaks.

Imagine that a new form of the Babylonian empire has turned your world upside-down. Imagine that all you have known is no more: your language forbidden, your religion banished. Everything you have known falls in those two categories. That void or abyss of personal history is the generational story of Armenian people after the 1915 genocide and the attempt to eliminate Armenian culture from Asia Minor. This reflects the situation for the Hebrew people in Babylon. To these people, Isaiah says, "Thus says God, the LORD, . . . I have given you as a covenant to the people, / a light to the nations, / to open the eyes that are blind, / to bring out the prisoners from the dungeon, / from the prison those who sit in darkness" (Isa. 42:7). More important still are these words, "See, the former things have come to pass, and new things I now declare" (v. 9). Given the bleak living conditions of the Hebrew people in Babylon, these words of promise bring good news!

Go back to verse 1. God speaks of sending a servant with the gentle and loving spirit of God. After all, the servant will not break a bruised reed (v. 3). This servant will bring justice in the earth (v. 4). This servant will bless God's people so that they become a light to the nations (v. 6). We too celebrate the good news: God's Anointed One brings liberation to people who sit in the darkness of captivity.

And Isaiah 49 speaks to people in captivity. While the people feel an overwhelming despair during this time in Babylon, Isaiah offers a simple message that we can summarize in one word: *Home.* God will establish the people in the land again. Home! "Sing for joy, O heavens, and exult, O earth. . . . For the Lord has comforted his people" (v. 13).

People today live in many forms of exile: as refugees from dictatorships or violence, as estranged from family, or in a prison of guilt or shame. We all live in the shadow of death. Our Advent-Christmas-Epiphany holy days proclaim that we meet God's generosity in the incarnate Christ. God's generous gift in Jesus offers liberation from despair, alienation, and separation. That generous gift is the key of life for which we thank God.

12 — Lost

Today's reflection begins with words from Isaiah 9:2-7. Take time to read the passage now. Two words associate themselves with this text: *lost* and *darkness*. We sometimes use the word *lost* to describe someone who is confused or perhaps deep in thought. We also use *lost* to describe an inability to control emotions ("X lost it and became angry"). *Lost* was once the title of a mysterious television program that piled puzzle upon mystery upon enigma upon conundrum. We describe lost treasures, lost souls, lost relatives,

Darkness, named in this week's antiphon, describes times of oppression and uncertainty as well as times of grief or tragedy. Two friends have written insightful books about spirituality and dark times. Steve Harper's *Talking in the Dark: Praying When Life Doesn't Make Sense* offers guidance for those times. More recently, Barbara Brown Taylor wrote *Learning to Walk in the Dark*, another guide when spirituality seems far from us. All these implications fit within the biblical notion of darkness.

Place the words *lost* and *darkness* on a mental shelf for a few moments as we dive into Isaiah 9:2-7, a traditional scripture passage read during Christmas Eve services. Even the least experienced reader feels moved to let these poetic cadences roll aloud. The passage begins with quiet light in the midst of fearful darkness: "The people who walked in darkness have seen a great light" (v. 2). The passage's momentum continues its steady gait as we hear the names of the child: "Wonderful Counselor, Mighty God, / Everlasting Father, Prince of Peace" (v. 6). Still the musical notes of the passage build in volume as we learn about the establishment of the throne of David with justice and righteousness (v. 7). Then the passage comes to a resolution with the final words, "The zeal of the LORD of hosts will do this."

George Frideric Handel used these words in the first portion of *Messiah*. Listening to *Messiah* may be part of your Advent-Christmas tradition or you may have opportunity to join a community chorus that sings this work. In that work a bass soloist sings, "The people that walked in darkness" and then comes a chorus, "For unto us a Child is born." These portions of *Messiah* follow an earlier bass solo based on Isaiah 60, which speaks of darkness covering the earth. Handel's musical genius helped us view this passage as a pointer to Christ's birth.

Long before Handel's association, another history surrounded Isaiah 9. Begin with Isaiah 9:1. Here we see a description of anguish. Assyrian armies have conquered the ancestral
territory of Zebulon (last son of Jacob and Leah) and Naphtali
(sixth son of Jacob and Bilhah). The tribal area of Zebulon fell
in the southern part of Galilee, between the Sea of Galilee and
the Mediterranean. Naphtali was also in the southern part of
Galilee. Both tribes essentially disappeared with the Assyrian
conquest and are now regarded as part of the Ten Lost Tribes of
Israel. Imagine being part of a tribe so lost and in darkness that
it simply disappeared!

But why? What happened? The king, the corrupt Ahaz,
sold out the territory by abandoning trust in God and rely-
ing on his own power. Instead of joining other nation-states in
opposing the Assyrians, Ahaz formed a partnership with Assyria
to assure that he would continue as king. After meeting with
Tiglath-pileser, king of Assyria, Ahaz returned to Jerusalem and
ordered the building of an altar modeled on the Assyrian altar.
Ahaz installed this new altar in the Temple. (Second Kings 16
describes the reign of Ahaz.) In all ways, Ahaz put himself above
the people he ruled and above the God who empowered him.
The Assyrians conquer Israel. Israel's people suffer because of
Ahaz's action. In the news stories of refugee camps, we can see a
suffering like that of old. The people now live in a psychological
state of darkness.

To the people who suffer from this military conquest, Isaiah
speaks the word of God. Light will drive out the darkness that
covers the land. Instead of diminishment, new generations will
come to life. Rather than the heavy weight of oppression, God
will bring lightness to the people. New birth and the wondrous
purity of a child will lead the people to justice and peace. To
people caught up in psychological darkness, this is good news!

Isaiah's text does not speak directly these next words, but I hear in them this promise: What was lost will be found. Not only will the lost be found, but the lost and those in darkness will be restored. God will restore and receive Zebulon and Naphtali and the other lost tribes of Israel. God will restore and receive us all, even those who are lost and those who walk in darkness and those who seem to straddle these positions. I base my belief on the final sentence of Isaiah 9:7: "The zeal of the LORD of hosts will do this." Another word for zeal is *passion*. God's passion is the transformation of this world, finding the lost, and bringing reconciliation to all people.

> **God, who are the people around me who travel in darkness? Who around me seeks light? How can I reach out to them? How will I pray for them today? Amen.**

11 — Key

Pray this antiphon:

> O Key of David and Scepter of the house of Israel, who opens and no one shuts, who shuts and no one opens: Come, and bring forth from prison the captive who sits in darkness and in the shadow of death.

Consider how a key functions. I think first of an entrance, much more than a basic door or a gated opening that is locked. This entrance exists on a gargantuan scale, dwarfing any normal door. In the doorway stands a foreboding keyhole to unlock the mechanism and gain access. An old-fashioned skeleton key rests by the opening. *Does it fit the lock? How would anyone know if it is the right key?* Pick up the key and try to fit it into the lock's passageway. If it seems to fit, then turn it to see whether the inner mechanism works. It works! The door opens, and all is well because the key works.

Think about another interpretation. The musician in me argues that I have described the wrong key and that I need to think about a musical key. After all, the Bible credits David as being a musician, and he needed to keep the strings on his harp in tune. We tune instruments by making sure one note is in pitch with another so that the notes of a musical scale find peace and harmony with one another. My maternal grandfather brought to this country an old zither that needed new strings and that had developed a small crack in the soundboard. No amount of turning the pegs could keep that instrument in tune to play properly, though I enjoyed strumming the zither. Some strings sang while others only buzzed out of tune.

Musical keys also generate various responses. We employ the same fingering on the piano when we play the C-major scale and the C-minor scale. However, our brains tell us that the two scales sound quite different. A melody in the key of B major sounds very different from the same melody in the key of G-sharp major. We will perceive many differences between the same melody played in B major if played in a minor key, such as F minor.

Maybe we should seek the key David once used. His psalms continue to inspire us to praise God. First Samuel 16 offers details from the life of David: "Whenever the evil spirit from God came upon Saul, David took the lyre and played it with his hand, and Saul would be relieved and feel better" (1 Sam. 16:23). David's harp became the key to releasing Saul from his manic darkness and his time in a spiritual prison.

Music can release and free us from negative emotions and responses. When I was a preschooler, my paternal grandfather taught me an Armenian song, which I understood as a reference to the moon and also to my mother because the Armenian word *lusin* (loo-seen) sounded much like my mother's first name, Lucy. I sat on the counter of the grocery store, and my grandfather and I sang. Later I learned that this song came from my grandfather's days as part of the Armenian resistance. Years later I learned the importance of song to every movement for liberation, including the American Revolution. I cannot imagine the American Civil Rights Movement or the Anti-Apartheid Movement in South Africa without song to organize and focus the effort.

We sing not only because we are happy, as one hymn suggests; we sing because music elevates and inspires. We sing in gratitude and praise. We sing of visions of better lives and better life. We sing of hope, and the very act of singing gives us the hope for which we sing. For a time, we set aside our burdens and open ourselves to the flow of God's love within us. Whether that lifting of burdens lasts seconds or minutes does not matter. What matters is that we experience a portion of God's love and grace, which is key to our life.

Notice what the hymns and carols of Christmas describe. Many of them point to the Nativity and then indicate something beyond the event. Consider how "Lift Up Your Heads, Ye Mighty Gates," an Advent hymn, points to our spiritual pilgrimage: "Thy Holy Spirit lead us on / until our glorious goal is won." "Away in a Manger" moves tenderly from past to present. "It Came upon the Midnight Clear" also offers a vision "when peace shall over all the earth its ancient splendors fling, / and the whole world send back the song which now the angels sing."

The antiphon promises that the Key of David is the song that liberates and sets free the prisoners.

> **Doors open and voices sing, loving God, and your love activates the power behind all. Praise to you and thanksgiving for the wonders of life! Amen.**

10 — A Nativity Set

I own five or six small Nativity sets and place them around my living space and workspace. These Nativity scenes succeeded an olive wood musical Nativity that my family had and lost somewhere along the way. I later visited The Upper Room museum's exhibit of Nativity sets from around the world and saw many creative expressions of God's love made visible in the vulnerable baby Jesus, Mary, and Joseph. The Nativity scenes include one from Hawaii made with a coconut shell and small starfish, a carved wood scene from Korea, a Nativity plate from El Salvador, a Honduran Nativity made from dried seedpods, a matchbox tableau from Peru, a Nigerian Nativity constructed from carved reeds, and an entire Nativity village of paper dolls that originated in Cold War Czechoslovakia. Robert Benson eventually wrote a book about the collection titled *The Night of the Child* (Upper Room Books), which includes representative photographs of the collection.

We see the Nativity frozen before us like a beloved old family photograph. The photograph has been handled and looked at so many times that we no longer need to look at it to envision the people gathered in it. The mental image of the Nativity scene mixes portions of Matthew and Luke. Tradition tells us that Saint Francis of Assisi put together the first Nativity to teach about the birth of Jesus.

Three things occur to me about Nativity sets. If you have a Nativity scene around you, I hope that you will look at it after reading this meditation.

The first observation is that Nativity scenes usually promote a sense of serenity. Mary either holds the baby in her arms or looks peacefully at the manger in which the baby rests. Joseph keeps his silence, but he also seems filled with an indescribable awe. The animals are all quite simultaneously at peace. If we see shepherds, they also express reverence and awe. If we see the magi, their expressions do not reveal the hardship they have experienced on the journey or the problems of dealing with King Herod. As with the others in this scene, the magi radiate tranquility. Is that not the quality we desire for ourselves, our families, our communities? And if we desire this for our communities, we also desire this serenity for our nation and for all other nations.

The second observation is the vulnerability present in the Nativity. We believe God became flesh, human, in this baby born in the very ordinary way in which all babies are born. God does not come fully formed as an adult. God does not begin with the power of might to force people to love; rather, God extends love, which is far more powerful than force and might. God comes as baby, as infant who will develop in all the normal ways humans develop from infancy to toddlerhood and childhood and on to adolescence and adulthood. We want to touch the baby, kiss him, protect him—as we would love, touch, kiss, and protect any newborn. We see the Nativity and the gentle sweetness of the mother and child, but we need also to remember that this is no ordinary newborn. This is God incarnate, God become human like us; we need to remember the importance of God's vulnerability.

My third consideration is easy to overlook. The Nativity crosses borders. These Nativity sets show us that the incarnation of God in Jesus does not stop at the borders of any nation. We talk a lot about global Christianity and the ways in which Christianity moves around the world, but any multinational or transnational Nativity collection will depict that global movement in a new way. We see how different cultures understand the significance of Christ.

While I like the serenity of a Bolivian wood carving of the Madonna and the novel construction of that Hawaiian Nativity, I want you to imagine the paper doll Nativity village from Czechoslovakia. Made in the 1950s, this set of paper dolls begins with the holy family; the shepherds and sheep and cows. Then it branches out to include a goose and a dusty baker and a farmworker and a woman who is caring for children and other characters who people this village. One character rushing to see the infant is an old man with a stein of beer. I like this Nativity because it embraces many of the people we say God loves. While not all inclusive, it is a start. Whenever you look at a Nativity scene, know that people around the world share the same love for Jesus Christ that you and I share.

Thank you, God, for becoming one of us and showing the whole world your love. May we delight in the mission of your transforming love. Amen.

9 — Open and Shut

As I read, prayed, and reflected on the antiphon, I kept returning to the words "who opens and no one shuts, who shuts and no one opens." Letting my imagination play with these words, I began a conversation with Jesus, which I do not intend to sound flippant. The church has a long tradition of guided prayers and prayer encounters with Christ. Ignatius of Loyola, for example, offered one set of prayer experiences, which were normally spread over thirty days. If you have sung "In the Garden," by C. Austin Miles, you have experienced a gentle guided prayer, especially when in the third stanza the hymn invites us to leave the garden and go about our mission. Such guided prayer intends to engage head and heart to grow more deeply in the love of Christ. You may have practiced such prayer in reading the Gospels during Holy Week and placing yourself among the disciples or with the crowd following Jesus. As you read the passages, you may have asked yourself, "How would I have responded if I had been with Jesus in the garden? What would I have done when they arrested Jesus?" After asking these sorts of questions during the reading, you may have found yourself seeing with the mind's eye the garden of Gethsemane and the people surrounding Jesus. Perhaps you may have seen yourself responding and, even more, the response of Jesus.

So my conversation with Jesus about the antiphon began in this way:

G: Who opens and no one shuts?

J: I do. You should know that. After all, I invited you into this conversation.

G: Yes, you did that, but I'm not sure about this opening and shutting business.

J: Are you forgetting your own time of exile? Not that you were cast out of anything, but you perceived yourself as excluded. I traveled with you before you felt that exclusion, sat beside you during your sense of exile, and then opened a way for you to come to your senses and enter anew the community of faith. I open the gate—not just for you, but all people—and I invite all people to come to a relationship with God, our Creator. People who seem like you and people who are on the other edge. People who seem to have stable lives and unstable lives, rich and poor, from all nations and places—I seek all to grow in a loving relationship with God.

G: OK, that I understand. Or I won't carp, even though that is my usual response.

J: You only complain and gripe about yourself. Not about others. But I'm interrupting. What else are you questioning?

G: This business of shutting and no one opens. What is that supposed to mean? Does that prayer mean that you let no one in? Or that once we're in, you don't let us out?

J: I don't eliminate the gift of free will. You will always have a choice to follow me. I don't lock in anyone. I welcome all. I show love to all. And while some people want to believe that I lock out some people, I don't do that. The Almighty One thinks that the world is worth redeeming—*all* of the world. Isn't that the message of John 3:16, my words that show up on so many signs? My mission has always been to redeem and transform people, to usher in God's age of peace and justice. I shut and no one opens has to do with defending the flock from the evil one. You hadn't thought of that, had you?

G: No, that's a new thought for me.

Shutting in has something to do with protecting or defending? Not quite what I expected to hear. Welcome and hospitality I understand, but the act of hospitality also defends and protects. Sometimes we forget that to welcome someone carries that double-edged meaning.

We want to welcome. We want people to join with us—in a cause, in an activity, in a church. But our responsibility does not stop in the act of invitation or welcome. When my family helped other Armenians to settle in the United States, the relationship did not end with finding housing or employment. The relationship continued with encouragement and nurture through the explanation of new customs and traditions. We recognize the crucial role of the sponsor in AA and other 12-Step groups. A sponsor helps a newcomer get sober and stay sober through the program. Sponsors do everything possible to help the newcomer succeed in the new way of living. That is a form of companionship and protection—another side of welcome.

We do not read much about the innkeeper who welcomed Joseph and Mary, but I imagine that he looked in on the Holy Family after Jesus' birth. I want to imagine that, in his own way, the innkeeper offered some protection to Joseph and Mary. May we extend hospitality to all people, knowing that Jesus Christ defends and protects all the flock.

> **Merciful God, may your welcome to us resonate through us to all people. May your love defend us from evil, and may you continue to offer us visions of the fullness of your reign on earth. We pray in the love of Jesus Christ. Amen.**

Questions for the Week

- How have you experienced a sense of being lost or exiled? What experience brought you to a point of returning to your senses and feeling at home?

- Have you experienced loss and grief in such a way that the world seemed dark? How did you experience a return of the light?

- What songs do you sing to elevate your spirits? Do you sing these songs alone or with others?

- What songs are important to sing as you celebrate the birth of Jesus? What songs do you sing to reinforce the message of Jesus?

- Do you have a Nativity set? Do you move the figures around and have the Magi travel closer to the stable as the time of Epiphany approaches? How do you let the figures teach you more about the birth of Jesus?

- How do you extend hospitality to strangers? to children? to the aged?

Christmas Week

O Dayspring, Brightness of the light eternal and Sun of
justice: Come, and enlighten those who sit in darkness
and in the shadow of death.

Christmas is here! The waiting is over. Christ is born among
us, for us! Christ is born in the world, for the world! How
are you celebrating this love of God?

Christians live with two differing biblical traditions related
to Christmas. The first tradition merges Luke 2:1-20 and Matthew 1:18–2:12. The second biblical tradition of Christmas
comes in the more symbolic text of John 1:1-18.

This antiphon spoke to me as I thought about these days in
the order of this book. Dayspring, light, Sun of justice all pointed
me toward the Gospel of John: "In the beginning was the Word,
and the Word was with God, and the Word was God. . . . The
light shines in the darkness, and the darkness did not overcome
it" (1:1, 5). We know that passage. Those of us who live in the
Northern Hemisphere identify with the proclamation of light as
the daylight hours shorten and the night lengthens. We love to
hear the reading of John 1. The words and phrases offer a mystical taste of creation, incarnation, and salvation. They extend a
poetic and symbolic witness to God's love, a witness that moves

beyond our ordinary experience and points to the extraordinary character of the event we celebrate in Jesus Christ. John's mystic revelation points us toward the heights of heaven.

When I read chapter 1 of John's Gospel and think of the portraits of Jesus' birth in Matthew and Luke, I sense a disconnect. John elevates the Incarnation to a mystical and spiritual plane while Matthew and Luke present the Incarnation in an everyday grittiness. The mystic in me thrills to John's Prologue, but I sense an equally intense awe as I consider the extraordinary wonder of Jesus' birth as narrated in Matthew and Luke.

Some of the most tenderhearted and loving preaching begins with the story of Jesus' birth. Both Martin Luther and Karl Barth, two of the more theologically dogmatic preachers in the history of the Protestant movement, preached lovingly evocative Christmas sermons that invited hearers to become open to God's love made visible. Collections of Luther's Christmas sermons are available and worth reading annually.

Here is a portion of a Christmas sermon preached in 1954 by Karl Barth to inmates in the state prison at Basel, Switzerland:

> This, then, is the Christmas story. You see, we cannot possibly hear this story and not look away from ourselves, from our own life with its cares and burdens. There he is, our great God and Saviour, and here we are, human beings, and now it is true that he is for me, is for us. Impossible to hear his story without hearing our own. . . . What shall we do now? Shall we continue in our old ways, in absentmindedness, in disbelief, perhaps in some lofty Christian sentiments? Or shall we awake and rise, set out on our journey and turn about? The angel of the Lord does not compel anybody. . . . We must willingly listen, and willingly participate. (*Deliverance to the Captives*, 26)

As Karl Barth noted, angels do not compel anyone; they offer an invitation. We always receive an invitation to respond to God's gift in Christ and to celebrate that grace throughout our lives.

As we celebrate the birth of Jesus, we see the others: shepherds, angels, animals, magi. In our mind's eye, they all come to the manger to see the baby, to worship, and to praise God for this gift of love visible. Then they depart as they came: angels, shepherds, magi, and last Joseph, Mary, and infant Jesus. We need them to leave the manger because we also need to leave the manger. We need to grow with Jesus. Like the magi, we need to go home another way, letting our love for God bless others through our actions. The days of Christmas and the movement toward Epiphany direct us away from comfortable routines to seek new ways to reach others and to show the love of God.

I hope you willingly keep your Christmas decorations up until January 6. When people ask if you have been too busy to take them down, you will some insight into how to respond.

Christmas is here! Christ is born among us, for us! Christ is born in the world, for the world! The story is good news! How are you celebrating this love of God?

8 — Candlelight

Did you participate in a Christmas Eve candlelight service? Some churches offer multiple candlelight services. My relatives in Brazil and my friends in South Africa do not have the Christmas Eve options that many churches in the United States offer. My relatives know only the later service at 11:00 PM because the earth's orbit around the sun gives the Southern Hemisphere more daylight in November–January than the Northern Hemisphere. Why do I refer to Christmas Eve in the Southern Hemisphere? What does this have to do with candlelight?

I believe it is important to remember that the celebration of Christ's birth takes place in different ways around the world. What seems traditional in New England may seem alien or strange in Texas or Brazil. The Korean or Armenian traditions will seem equally foreign to many New Englanders. Far better to remember that all these traditions make known a critical reality of life: God's gracious love made known to all people in the incarnation of Jesus Christ.

Candlelight services of worship tend toward the quiet side. Even churches that practice exuberant styles of worship generally offer reflective worship as we approach midnight on Christmas Eve. We go to candlelight services at twilight or in the dark. We follow different liturgies and then, usually in response to a sermon or prior to the singing of a final hymn, we light candles, sharing from one candle to another. We may reflect on John 1:5: "The light shines in the darkness, and the darkness did not overcome it." We may sing softly and perhaps unaccompanied "Silent Night" or another reverent hymn. The pastor may encourage us to leave the service in silence.

Sometimes these moments of silence are the only still times our packed Christmas holiday schedules offer. Our days become so full of events and preparation for events, for guests arriving or for travel to see family, that we feel overscheduled and overwhelmed. We have few moments for quiet reflection; we often arrive at Christmas too full and too stressed to recognize the wonder of the celebration. Christmas Eve services can provide a moment of stillness to nurture our spirits and to rekindle our sense of awe as we witness and celebrate God's love anew.

Why am I writing about Christmas Eve candlelighting and stillness when Christmas is here or perhaps you are reading this meditation on the day after Christmas? People need times of stillness each day. Some people object to moments of silence. One of my friends always objects to the idea of stillness in the day. "I can't be silent. It brings a feeling of fear." Notice that I am writing about stillness. Stillness may mean a time of sitting in silence, but it may mean listening without distraction to a piece of music or focusing on a photograph or other piece of art even while sounds occur in the background. Stillness may be a time of prayer or a time of reading or listening to a Bible passage. In the stillness we may come to grips with an inner wound that requires healing, a place easy to miss in the busyness of our lives.

Two scripture passages come to mind regarding stillness. Near the close of Psalm 46 we read the words "Be still, and know that I am God!" (v. 10). Sometimes our activities clutter life so much that we forget the great nature of God and fall into the trap of thinking that everything depends on us and our doing all things. We become so caught up in these activities that we involuntarily believe that the world cannot go on without us. I use the word *involuntarily* because if asked about this, we all say, "Oh no, God is sovereign." Our actions sometimes show the opposite. Be still, and listen to God in the moment.

The second passage of scripture concerns an event in the life of Jesus recorded in Matthew 8:23-27; Mark 4:35-41; and Luke 8:22-25. Look up these passages in which Jesus calms a storm. Each version offers the same story: A storm threatens to capsize the boat while Jesus and the disciples are crossing the sea. The disciples waken Jesus because they fear they will drown. While the versions in Matthew and Luke say that Jesus rebuked the wind and the water, in the Gospel of Mark, Jesus addresses the water and says, "Peace! Be still!" (Mark 4:39). While addressed to the sea, I think Jesus spoke indirectly to the disciples and therefore to us. Be still and silence the inner storm.

Be still. Despite the activities, seek quiet. You may discover a rich tapestry of love and compassion within yourself that has been overcrowded by activity. You may discover a surprising sense of joy and peace.

Guide me, great God, to the still places of life. If I am not comfortable with silence, overcome my fear and help me to be still. In the stillness may I come to a new quality of relationship with you and discover some facets of life hidden by activities. Help me to acknowledge quiet as a friend and stillness a comfort as I hear the voice of Jesus say, "Be still," I pray. Amen.

7 — Children

We usually refer to Clement Clarke Moore's poem as "'Twas the Night before Christmas," which he titled "A Visit from St. Nicholas." Moore's poem shapes a number of our Christmas traditions. We learn names of eight reindeer and meet Saint Nick with a peddler's sack. Early in the poem we read, "The children were nestled all snug in their beds." Thanks to illustrated books and our imaginations, we see two or three children huddled in a featherbed and covers pulled up. Perhaps one child's eyes are open. Moore offered us a portrait of anticipation in that poem and then brought resolution to the little drama.

Some adults say, "Christmas is for children. Our children are grown and live far away. We're too old for all that stuff." That statement came in response to questions about Christmas gifts, decorations, and plans. To a degree, that statement is accurate, especially the way corporations market Christmas to consumers. If we believe the seasonal commercials, the purpose of Christmas is to buy children all the toys they desire and for adults a time to buy jewelry and cars. While the commercials may try to convince us, people know that Christmas has a very different meaning or purpose. Those who do not follow Christ find ways to celebrate the Christmas holiday. Beyond the surface of our usual seasonal behavior, people know that Christmas is not just for children and certainly not merely a time to buy stuff.

I prayed, "O Dayspring, Brightness of the light eternal and Sun of justice." Children became part of my reflection; something about children kept nudging me in the prayer. I found myself saying that I love my children, my family. I try to do all that I can to guide them toward maturity. What more can I do? And the word *justice* seemed to leap from the prayer and stay in my awareness so that I began to join the two words: children and justice. What can we do for them? What are we doing for them? What are we doing to improve conditions so that the children will inherit a more just and loving world?

During the last few years, I have served as pastor to three small congregations. Each church has dwindled in membership, which mirrors problems in the neighborhoods and within church life. Two congregations are set in mill villages, housing developments built by textile mill owners for the factory workers. The mills closed thirty or more years ago, and the neighborhood churches continue despite the shifting demographics and diminishing economics. They face a variety of problems that range from unemployment to drug and alcohol abuse and other issues. A third congregation is set in relatively open country. Here again the area had depended upon textile mills so that unemployment continues to be a major issue. An elementary school sits across the road from this church. Despite dwindling numbers, each church sees children as a vital part of mission and ministry. One church provides school supplies and backpacks at the start of the school year and then restocks those supplies after Christmas and again at Easter. Another church supplies weekend food toward the end of each month and works to provide meals for families. Another church tutors children in the neighborhood school and began involvement with Bread for the World to seek change in governmental food policies.

"Why are you doing this?" asked a parent who was picking up supplies.

"Our church believes God wants to transform the world. This is how we can help God," replied the church member.

"We can't pay you back. What are you getting out of this?"

"You don't pay us back. God loves us and wants us to show love to the world. That's all there is to it."

Now that dialogue has no veneer of sophistication to make it seem more significant. Those simple statements sound genuine and real to me. We act out of our convictions. As we continue in the days after Christmas, simple mission and ministry seem right to me. We say that the light of Christ came into the world and that the darkness cannot extinguish that light. We make that light visible through our ministries with children. Children are in need here, there, everywhere. We see the need in our home areas, in the rural areas of Haiti, and the urban neighborhoods of Aleppo.

God, we have more questions than answers. We witness world events that we don't support. How can we bring change? Where do we start? Show us the way. Amen.

6 — A Story

The many activities of the Christmas season test our mental, physical, and spiritual endurance. How do we recognize the hidden stress and seek healing? Some people state that they hate what Christmas does to them. We may feel tempted to become a misanthrope, someone who hates humanity.

I write a blog titled *This, That, and T'Other from Ms. Anne Thrope's Coffee Club*. The imaginary setting is an independent coffee shop where people drink tiny cups of Armenian coffee, play backgammon and chess, eat Armenian and Middle Eastern pastries, and relax. Photographs of William Saroyan, an American novelist, playwright, and short story writer born of Armenian parents, decorate the main room.

Why name my blog Ms. Anne Thrope's? A professor in an American literature course required the class to read *The Turn of the Screw*, a ghost story with psychological overtones, written by Henry James and published in 1898. The professor thought it a good introduction to the author. *The Turn of the Screw* features adults, two children, perhaps a ghost or two, and the narrator, who serves as the children's governess. Everyone in the book is named except the governess. When the novel was published, the anonymity of the governess added to the suspense. I still remember the exam question: "If you could give a name to the governess in *The Turn of the Screw*, what would it be? Why?"

I was not prepared for that question and wrote only "Ms. Anne Thrope"—no additional commentary. The stunned professor gave me full credit. Instead of hating humanity, Ms. Anne Thrope of the Coffee Club is a warmhearted person. She may even be a Methodist of some sort. Here's the story:

After Christmas, people packed into Ms. Anne Thrope's Coffee Club. They played chess and backgammon, talked about families and politics, and kept the staff busy. The previous week, people had been agitated due to shopping for last-minute Christmas gifts. We have the same pattern every year. Ms. Anne Thrope gets sad because the business is off, but she enjoys the conversations the week after Christmas. This year was different. Ms. Anne seemed curt with customers and jumped on staff for small things she usually overlooked. Strawberry Mgrdichian, the other full-time employee, and I tried to protect Ms. Anne and the customers from one another.

"Ms. Anne, let's take a break," I said, nudging her toward the back room.

She shook her head and said, "Some days it isn't worth coming to the shop."

"We're doing good business. Lots of customers. People want to talk, drink coffee, eat *paklava* (a Western Armenian word for pastry known as baklava), drink more coffee. It's a good time. Here, let me make you some Armenian coffee."

"Thanks, I could use a cup, but I don't want my grounds read. It's too much for me."

"The customers are too much? It's the season of good cheer. Enjoy it—they'll be back to complaining soon. You do seem sad this year."

"Always I remember William Saroyan. He was an old man when I knew him. He used to laugh—big laugh—and say silly things like 'Everybody has got to die, but I always thought I would be an exception to that rule' and he'd laugh so loud you had to laugh with him. Things like that. Now let me say that I'm healthy. But Christmas reminds me of Saroyan and other people who have died. I'm getting old. I remember family members who aren't around. This year seems harder than usual. I didn't really enjoy Christmas."

"I imagine that you have good memories of Mr. Saroyan and many other people, Ms. Anne. That's a gift."

"Maybe, but it's a hard gift. I saw an article online about post-Christmas sadness. That's probably what I have.

"I didn't do everything I wanted to do. I didn't do much at all. My kids came, but they seemed preoccupied before they arrived and my grandson got sick the night before Christmas Eve. Pretty sad, he was," she continued. "And nobody put a brand new car under my tree. Not that I wanted one, but it's such a fantasy. So much fake stuff we expect to please us."

"Sometimes we miss truth in front of us because we're looking too hard at the past. But maybe that's why we celebrate Christmas. To remember that God provides many gifts to each of us over a lifetime. To remember the birth of Jesus and what that means—because it is a gift of love." I was not sure if these words were right for the moment.

"I know that. I'm tired and Christmas happened too quickly for me. Bang! It was here! Bang! It was gone! And somehow I feel like I missed it."

"Be gentle with yourself, Ms. Anne. Christmas is hard on everyone because of all the expectations people have. You know—the perfect tree, the perfect decorations, perfect meal, the perfect setting, the perfect gift. We get slammed by this illusion of perfection because none of us can pull it off, and it's a long way from the birth of Jesus. You remember what Saroyan wrote in *The Time of Your Life*? I can't quote it exactly, but he said to seek goodness and when you find it, bring it out of its hiding place. Sounds a little like Jesus and what he said about the kingdom of God and the mustard seed."

"Sometimes you sound like a preacher. Not a very good one but OK. You make me laugh. You think I should be gentle with myself? Sure, why not?"

God, sometimes it's hard to be kind and gentle with myself. Remind me that gentleness is a fruit of the Spirit, and that it means to be tender and compassionate and loving—with others and with myself. Amen.

5 — A Candle

Usually we light candles for festive occasions. We light candles on cakes to celebrate birthdays. We make wishes and blow out those candles. Sometimes those birthday wishes come true. At marriage ceremonies we light unity candles to represent the joining of two families into one. We delight in these times; the candles seem to reflect our own sense of lightness. At other times a lit candle reminds us of a solemnity or holiness surrounding an occasion. Some churches give families a special candle to light each year on the anniversary of a baptism and as a way to talk about and remember the significance of that baptism. On Easter churches may light the great Paschal candle to remind us of the light of Christ.

During the various services of worship from Advent to Epiphany, we have probably witnessed the lighting of many candles. We light two candles on the altar, and these may symbolically represent the humanity and the divinity of Christ. We light the four candles of an Advent wreath. Three of the Advent candles may be purple or blue and one is pink. Some people identify these candles with hope, love, joy, and peace. On Christmas Eve we often light a tall white Christ candle, which reminds us that the darkness does not overcome the light. In that same Christmas Eve service, we may also hold and light smaller candles with drip protectors or we may use battery-powered candles or even glow sticks to remember that the light shines in the darkness, and the darkness does not overcome it. Perhaps we sang a portion of Mary Lu Walker's hymn "Light the Advent Candle" each Sunday after lighting candles on the Advent wreath, or perhaps we sang "Silent Night" by candlelight on Christmas Eve.

Imagine a candle standing in front of you. Take a deep breath, and invite Christ to light a path for you. Now light the imaginary candle. Let it burn.

In your mind's eye, look at the candle that you have lit. What is its appearance? Is it standing straight? Does wax drip? Some theologians and teachers of symbolic meaning point out that a lit candle will include three parts: wick, wax, and flame. These theologians say that the wick represents the soul of Christ, the wax represents his humanity, and the flame his soul. It reminds me of teachings that employed the three leaves of a shamrock to speak of the Trinity. If this interpretation of the candle parts serves as a holy nudge for you, then remember it.

As I look at my imaginary candle, I recall my participation in a small group that opened each weekly gathering by lighting a candle and letting the candle burn throughout our time together. Our gathering words were always a variation of these sentences: "We light this candle as a reminder of the light of Christ, and we remember that our time together is holy time. Come, Holy Spirit." When our conversation moved into matters of justice, we began lighting a candle that a group participant brought from a trip to South Africa. This candle, wrapped with a small strand of barbed wire, stood for compassion, peace, and justice. Another name for that barbed-wire-covered candle was love.

We recall the saying that it is better to light a candle than to curse the darkness. These words surface whenever a matter of injustice comes before us. We seek solutions to current problems rather than complain and add to the problems. As baptized Christians, we are called to renounce the evil and injustice of the world and to proclaim the love of God in Jesus Christ to all people. We need not curse the darkness or stumble because of it. The light resides within us—the radiant love of Christ.

Do you remember the imaginary candle that you lit while reading this meditation? It burns still. Keep in mind that it is the light of Christ, and the darkness cannot extinguish it. Do you still see the light?

Lord Christ, you are the living light, the light of the world, the light eternal. Provide light for our journeys that we may be filled with love and compassion. Keep our motives and mission transparent so that your love will radiate through us to others. Amen.

Questions for the Week

- What has been your experience with Christmas Eve candlelight services?

- As you prepare resolutions and goals for the coming year, how are you adding spiritual practices to those goals?

- When have you experienced sadness or grief or anger in the days after Christmas? What evoked those feelings? How did they affect you? How were your feelings transformed and your balance restored?

- What was your reaction to the imaginary candle (meditation 5)? Have you participated in a small group that lit a candle to begin its time together? How can a candle serve to remind you of Christ?

- How are you involved in ministries with children? How are you showing children the love of Christ? What are you doing to serve the cause of justice?

Epiphany Week

O King of the Gentiles and their Desired One, Cornerstone that makes both one: Come, and deliver us whom
you formed out of the dust of the earth.

Stepping into a new year usually brings moments of reflection and time to make plans and perhaps resolutions for the
unfolding year. Christmas seems long ago. Many of us recall the
major events in the nation and the world, such as the formation
of a new government or the explosion of a long-dormant vol-
cano or an act of war. We consider other transitions, especially
the deaths of celebrities and those of our acquaintance, but we
also remember and celebrate births, marriages, and festive family or community events. We may pull out a computer file or a
paper folder that contains our resolutions for the previous year
and check to see which resolutions we fulfilled. We may take
time to write resolutions for the coming year. These resolutions
can motivate us to join with others in new fitness regimens at
the gym or to communicate more often with distant family and
friends or to read the Bible more reflectively throughout the year
or to begin a Wesleyan-style time of weekly fasting and prayer
from Thursday afternoon until Friday afternoon. A fresh year
and a relatively blank calendar invite us to begin new practices.

While we think about a fresh year, I dare to offer some reflections that grow from a prayer associated with December 22, to write about the hopes contained in that prayer, and to write a little about Epiphany and Armenian Christmas.

I invite you to pray the antiphon that opens this week. Where does this prayer direct your attention? The prayer reminds me of a passage in First Peter: "Come to [Christ], a living stone . . . and like living stones, let yourselves be built into a spiritual house, to be a holy priesthood" (2:4-5). To join in regular daily and weekly spiritual practices creates in us a deeper desire to become like Christ, like living stones. Those practices include daily Bible reading and contemplation or reflection on the reading, prayer for others and self, reading and reflecting on Christian literature, involvement in public worship, participation in discipleship or accountability groups, fasting, and more.

We employ these purposeful practices to become like Jesus Christ. Jesus' life demonstrated what writers would later call the fruit of the Spirit: love, joy, peace, patience, kindness, generosity, faithfulness, gentleness, and self-control. (See Galatians 5:22-23.) As we continue to open ourselves to God's grace, those gifts will flourish within us. that occurs when we place Christ the cornerstone at the center of our discipleship. Practicing the way of discipleship and demonstrating the fruit of the Spirit give way to action in, around, and throughout the world. Christmas moves us toward Epiphany and a remembrance of the magi, who traveled to see the Christ and then went home by another way. God offers each of us an alternate route as we travel the world.

Throughout this book I refer to Armenia, a small landlocked nation of Asia Minor located between the Black Sea and the Caspian Sea. The country bridges Asia and Europe, offering the strengths and wisdom of the many peoples who travel through the region. My family came to the United States from Turkey in the days of the Ottoman Empire. They arrived by circuitous routes. They escaped the genocide of Armenian people, a historic event denied by some and debated by others. The killings and the efforts to eliminate all signs of the culture have shaped the lives of Armenians ever since.

It is impossible to separate Armenian culture from the Armenian Church. Armenia became a nation dedicated to Christ in the year 301. Armenian practices of faith continue through generations of ancestral tradition. The Sunday liturgy of the Armenian Church, known as the badarak, is essentially the same today as it was in the twelfth century and in the eighth century. The language used is Armenian—no matter the location of the congregation. The liturgy, the prayers, and the sacrament of Holy Communion do not vary from week to week or congregation to congregation. As a child, I found these church services boring because I did not understand the medieval Armenian language or the liturgical action. As I matured and learned more, I came to appreciate the rich spiritual tapestry of the Armenian liturgy.

Armenians celebrate Easter at the same time as the Western Church, but the timing of Christmas differs. Prior to the fourth century, Christians celebrated the birth of Jesus on January 6. Throughout the Roman Empire, the church changed the date from January 6 to December 25 to take advantage of the established Saturnalia, a pagan celebration that ended around December 25. The Roman Church then declared the date of Epiphany as January 6. Armenians had no Saturnalia tradition and ignored this shift. To this day, Armenians celebrate three events on January 6: the birth of Jesus, the Epiphany or Theophany (meaning revelation of God and in Armenian Astvats-a-haytnyut-yoon), and the baptism of Jesus by John. The January 6 service includes a Blessing of Water liturgy to remember the baptism of Christ and the baptisms of the faithful who are invited to drink some of the holy water at the close of the service.

I write and talk about exiled Armenian culture from time to time. People know little about Armenia and find this topic fascinating. To me this is simply a tiny snapshot of a much larger picture given by God of a world filled with wonder, with different histories and cultures and perspectives. May God help us see the importance and gifts of all people and all cultures.

Epiphany invites us to move outward in mission and ministry. I may be guilty of stretching the meaning of the magi's journey home, but I do believe their return points to our outreach. We do not come to Christ and leave unchanged. Christ touches us, and nothing remains the same. We invite, teach, pray, support, sustain, nurture, assist, and encourage others.

God's peace to you as you continue the journey to Epiphany and beyond.

4 — Magi

What images come to mind when you think of the magi? You probably sang "We Three Kings," written by the Episcopal priest John H. Hopkins Jr. This hymn, probably written for a family Christmas pageant in 1857, shapes the way many people understand the ones that the New Revised Standard Version of the Bible calls "wise men." Long before Hopkins wrote his hymn, these visitors to the Holy Family received names. Three names stand out: Melchior, Gaspar, and Balthasar. Tradition also adds further identification so that Balthasar comes from Arabia, Melchior from Persia, and Gaspar from India.

We meet these travelers in Matthew 2:1-12. Consider reading this passage as part of your devotional time. Matthew does not tell us how many traveled to see the baby, only that they brought three gifts. Matthew refers to them as magi (persons understood to be priests of Zoroaster, the founder of the Persian religion Zoroastrianism that studied the stars.) Matthew writes that the magi enter a house and see the child with Mary. Then they offer their gifts of gold, frankincense, and myrrh. After the visit, they return to their own country.

While we may dismiss astrology and the position of stars as influences on our lives, we can learn from the magi to pay attention to the events going on around us. Years later, Jesus responded to those who demanded a heavenly sign, "When it is evening, you say, 'It will be fair weather, for the sky is red.' And in the morning, 'It will be stormy today, for the sky is red and threatening.' You know how to interpret the appearance of the sky, but you cannot interpret the signs of the times" (Matt. 16:2-3). We cannot remain oblivious to events around us; we need to pay attention.

The magi acted upon the information they had. They went on a quest, trusting that they had interpreted the signs rightly and that God would lead them to the right place. Trust remains key to their journey. Sometimes our actions demonstrate a lack of trust in God that all shall be well. We give in to our worries and fears. We try to manipulate people or manipulate God. We bargain with God. The journey across Persia to Bethlehem was no simple or peaceful camel ride. They traveled at least one thousand miles through areas controlled by bandits. I imagine that they wanted to quit often, and yet they held on to the greater vision that encouraged them through daily hardships.

The magi gave themselves fully to the moment. As we read Matthew 2, we see the magi enter the house and kneel before the baby. They offer their gifts and then leave. They do not cling to Mary and baby Jesus. Their visit is enough. They neither linger nor hurry. As we give ourselves to tasks at hand, can we also offer our gifts and do what is necessary and then take our leave?

Matthew narrates, "Having been warned in a dream not to return to Herod, they left for their own country by another road" (2:12). The magi acted upon the nudges they received.

As I wrote in an earlier meditation, I believe that God offers us nudges in our sleeping dreams, but I believe that we also receive nudges while we are awake. Those nudges take the form of random thoughts that come from nowhere and bid us to telephone an old friend, visit a friend in the assisted living center, pray for a person, send an encouraging note to someone in the community. We do well to pay attention to these seeming bits of random energy and act on them.

The magi went home. Unlike children's books that tell us what happened to every character, Matthew does not reveal the close of the story for the magi. They move forward on life's journey, and I trust that God continued to shape their lives. In our interactions with others who come and go in and out of our lives, we bless them and let them go. We do this as our children mature but also in our work settings and churches and other community groups. People become part of our circle for a time, and then they move on. We choose to hold on to a relationship, sometimes clinging with all the negative aspects of that word, or to bless and release. The warning in that dream to the magi conveyed both blessing and release. So may it be for us.

Today brings its special treasures, God. May we notice and open your gifts in the grace of Christ. Amen.

3 — Books and Reading

I hope it does not surprise you that I suggest reading as a spiritual practice. Writers read. Editors read. When editors and writers and publishers meet together, they moan and complain that people no longer read. Different studies suggest that as many as 124% of the population has not read a book since leaving high school. I confess that 124% is purposely inaccurate, but a sizable portion of the population of the United States may not have bought a book since leaving school. I hope that these non-buyers hold library cards.

As a pastor, I invite people to sit and read the Gospel of Mark in the same way that they would read a novel—from beginning to end. A person can read Mark in about an hour. Seeing the whole of this Gospel offers a much broader experience than reading three verses here and twelve verses there. Those who read through the book gain a new perspective on Jesus' mission and ministry. I have also recommended books to church members who wanted to grow as Christ-followers. Many thanked me because they found the books helpful. Several said that no pastor had ever recommended reading to them.

I come from a ministerial line that includes John Wesley. Wesley claimed to be a person of "one book," meaning the Bible. Wesley read and studied the Bible daily, but he also read other books, particularly in the area of Christian devotion and prayer and spiritual practice. Wesley wrote and published many books and pamphlets. He also published the works of other authors without getting permission to publish. (Our understanding of author rights has changed tremendously since Wesley's era.) The early Methodist circuit-riding preachers included Wesleyan pamphlets and books for sale in their gear. The books and pamphlets read and published by John Wesley are part of what I describe as spiritual reading.

By spiritual reading, I mean the Bible plus the following: the history and teachings of the church, the thoughts and writings of those we consider saints or saintly people, and the practical reflection on various aspects of Christian discipleship. We read these as a way to nourish Christian faith and action, to generate deeper prayer and devotion, and to encourage action for the sake of God's reign.

Reading is a countercultural experience in our noisy times. In reading we gain quiet time for reflection on the deep matters of life. By reading, I mean the use of a physical book or electronic device rather than an audiobook. Narrators of audiobooks offer their own interpretations through vocal inflection, and these books push us forward to completion.

Spiritual reading develops its own speed, and we read at a different pace than when we skim the Internet or a newspaper or read a detective novel. Spiritual reading will nudge us to digest the text on our own schedule. To a young adult I recommended *The Sayings of the Desert Fathers*, compiled by Benedicta Ward. That reader has set out on a two-year reflective journey on the topics addressed by these fourth- and fifth-century Christians. She has read less hastily and more reflectively. Taking the time to digest these books also goes contrary to cultural expectations. We read these books so that they will help us to mature or to change. Our best growth happens slowly.

Reading allows us to gain wisdom from others' experience and thought. We may learn from the conversion experience of Augustine of Hippo or the prison experience of Dietrich Bonhoeffer. We discover that we are not alone with our questions; others have wrestled spiritually with similar questions. The writings of others may not solve our inner struggle, but the work will guide and encourage us on our journey.

Engaging in conversation with others about a book will aid the digestion of a particular work. You may want to start a small group to focus on spiritual reading. Hearing others respond to a book will bear out our own response and will help connect us in new ways to others who seek life in Christ. Working through a book with a small group stimulates learning and fellowship.

Take time to browse in your church library. Ask your pastor to recommend books. Turn off the television, and enjoy thirty minutes of spiritual reading every day.

God, it seems that books are gifts from one generation to another, and they serve as beacons along the way. It's wonderful that the many books of the Bible stir us to faith and that we received the Word from you. In gratitude for the gift of reading and the gift of books. Amen.

2 — Fasting

I exercise at the local YMCA, a relatively longstanding practice. In the month of January, people crowd the Y and other gyms, resolved to lose weight or to get in better physical condition during the coming year. They may have gained weight during the Thanksgiving-Christmas-New Year festivities. Some even try to fast for a day or two, thinking that this practice may change their metabolism. This meditation does not approach fasting as a weight loss program.

Fasting is a spiritual discipline that seems the topic of more joking than genuine practice. As Ash Wednesday approaches, we hear comments about fasting in the form of giving up chocolate for the season of Lent. In my book *A World Worth Saving*, I devote one chapter to fasting. There I suggested that we give up a non-caring attitude or fast from apathy. In this meditation I invite you to consider the purpose of fasting.

All spiritual practices open us to formation in Christ's image. Just as we exercise the body to stay fit, we undertake a variety of spiritual exercises to grow and to mature as Christian disciples. Primary practices for such growth include daily Bible reading and reflection, prayer, participation in public worship, frequent Communion, and fasting. Jesus himself spoke about fasting in the Sermon on the Mount, giving plain instructions in Matthew 6:16-18 concerning appearance and attitude during the fast.

So what is fasting? The most basic fast is to abstain from food and drink (or food only or from a particular type of food) for a period of time and to combine that time with prayer. Fasting provides a way to control our appetites—physical, emotional, and spiritual. We may choose to fast to demonstrate love for God, to seek forgiveness for a wrong, to seek an answer or guidance about a perplexing matter. Within our fasting resides the acknowledgment of God as the source of all facets of our nourishment.

Beyond avoiding food or drink, fasting becomes a way for us to set aside, for a defined time or for the remainder of our lives, some activity or action that has become habitual to us. We may choose to fast for a week from our compulsion to be early for all meetings or to fast for a month from Facebook or other social media. We may choose to fast from angry reactions brought on by problems beyond our control. We may choose to fast from apathy and instead seek solutions to large social problems. Our fast may call us to go on a solitary weekend retreat. Or our fast may embrace an unplugging of television and other electronic stimulation for a defined time.

Fasting is a form of self-denial, and that runs counter to much in contemporary culture. Many people feel entitled to have what they want. Their motto could be "I want what I want when I want it." Culture in the United States seems built on a need for instant gratification. The ease of credit plus fear of economic uncertainty coupled with a sense of scarcity work together to increase an insecurity that seeks relief in instant gratification. Paul described such gratification in Philippians 3:19 when he wrote about the importance of following his own example rather than the larger non-Christian culture: "Their god is the belly . . . their minds are set on earthly things."

I invite you to observe the fast, to set aside time each week to abstain from food or drink and to use that time to seek God's wisdom. John Wesley, for example, fasted from after high tea on Thursdays until high tea on Fridays. Our own fast could begin Thursday afternoon and end Friday afternoon.

In a sermon titled "On Fasting," Basil the Great (330–79) stated the following:

> Fasting gives birth to prophets and strengthens the powerful; fasting makes lawgivers wise. Fasting is a good safeguard for the soul, a steadfast companion for the body, a weapon for the valiant, and a gymnasium for athletes. Fasting repels temptations, anoints unto piety; it is the comrade of watchfulness and the artificer of chastity. In war it fights bravely, in peace it teaches stillness. (*Orthodox Tradition*, vol. XXIII, no. 3, 2006, 6–16)

Notice all the positive qualities Basil attributes to fasting! Fasting repels temptation and safeguards the soul. It anoints us with godliness and teaches peace. Basil correctly identifies fasting as a companion of watchfulness, a quality Jesus emphasized in several passages of scripture. (See, for example, Matthew 24:36-44; Luke 12:35-40; Luke 21:34-36.)

Fasting is not a hunger strike nor is it a time to brag to others and proudly say, "I am fasting from XYZ." We follow the teaching of Jesus to go about life as usual and to let our fast be seen solely by God. Nothing else matters.

God, I know that you do not care for dismal or gloomy saints. Help me to fast with joy, knowing that the reward is greater than any meal I may experience. Amen.

1—Baptism

Remember you are baptized, and be thankful. My church home, the United Methodist Church, tends at this time of year toward a service of covenant renewal with a liturgy that also remembers one's baptism. The Armenian Apostolic Orthodox Church, my other church, celebrates Jesus' baptism at the same time that it celebrates Christmas. I appreciate the fact that at the start of the year, both churches emphasize the importance of baptism.

Armenians generally baptize infants. It is the sacrament of initiation into the Christian community. My baptism took place at Saint Gregory the Illuminator Armenian Apostolic Church in Philadelphia, Pennsylvania. I do not remember what happened, but I have witnessed other baptisms in the Armenian tradition and have baptized others in the Wesleyan tradition. In the Armenian baptism three sacraments take place. The priest baptizes the infant with water, anoints the infant with holy oil (known as holy chrism or muron) in the sacrament of Chrismation, and gives the infant her or his first Communion. During Chrismation, the Armenian priest anoints and blesses the infant's head, eyes, nose, mouth, ears, chest, arms, feet, and back. The church understands the anointing of Chrismation as a sealing with the Holy Spirit, giving the child spiritual strength.

"Remember your baptism, and be thankful," we say in baptismal renewal services, or perhaps we say, "Remember that you are baptized, and be thankful." The instruction does not ask that we remember each specific moment of our baptism but to recall that we have been baptized and to remember the significance of that act. What should we remember about baptism?

In baptism we become part of the body of Christ. We are incorporated into this process of discipleship that moves throughout history and around the world. Our baptism took place in a specific place, from which we may have long ago moved; yet, our baptism is into the body of Christ, a mystical event that transcends our place and our time. People frequently limit their understanding of baptism to a particular congregation, but every congregation baptizes and incorporates people into the far greater body of Christ.

In baptism we become aware of our relationship with God, and we begin the lifelong process of Christian discipleship. Baptism is not the goal of evangelism; discipleship is the goal of evangelism. Our baptisms lead us to open ourselves even more to God's love. If we were baptized as infants, we moved from the basic infant nursery where people loved and cared for us to an elementary understanding of God's love. From that elementary understanding we began to ask questions and discovered new answers in the process of confirmation. As adolescents we may have redefined our Christian discipleship and moved to a commitment to seek justice in the world for the sake of Christ. As adults we began to discover fresh ways to pray, new spiritual disciplines, and broader dimensions of Christian witness. We were baptized, and the journey began.

As we remember our baptism, we acknowledge God's action in our lives long before our awareness of God's presence. Theologian John Wesley identified a process of God's action in our lives as prevenient or preparing grace, justifying grace, and sanctifying grace. Prevenient simply means "coming before." We look back at our lives and realize that God loved us before we were aware of God and before we made any commitment to follow the way of Christ. Justifying grace refers to forgiveness and freedom from the power of sin, as well as new relationships with God and with others. Sanctifying grace makes possible our growth as disciples and leads us to inward and outward holiness. As we progress from baptism to maturity as Christian disciples, we move toward holiness and love in all facets of life. Whether we were baptized as infants or as older children or as adults, we

102 In Days to Come

can look back and understand that God's love surrounded us before we were conscious of that love.

The focus of this meditation concerns baptism, but I invite you to remember the last portion of the sentence about baptism: "Remember . . . and be thankful." Be thankful. Be thankful that you are part of the body of Christ. Be thankful for the spiritual adventure of life in Christ. Be thankful for the ways in which you understand God's love. Be thankful on waking each morning for a fresh awareness of God's love. Be thankful for the sustaining support of God throughout each day. Be thankful and rejoice in the knowledge of God's love in the incarnation of Jesus Christ. Thanks be to God!

> God, the water of baptism is such a simple gift, and it brings us to a new way of living. Our lives are in your love. Thank you. Amen.

Questions for the Week

- Amid violence, how do you bear witness or act for peace?

- How have you identified with the journey of the magi? What hardships do you imagine the magi experienced on their journey to Bethlehem and their return home? What do you believe encouraged them to continue on the journey? What encourages you to continue as a disciple?

- Have you considered the importance of reading as a Christian spiritual practice? Have you joined with others to discuss books about Christian discipleship? How do you think reading and conversation about the books will help you grow in love?

- Think of the last baptism you witnessed. What do you most remember about the ritual and about the people? How was this sacrament a time of teaching and witnessing to faith?

- Fasting seems to be the most difficult spiritual practice because it runs contrary to our expectations. When and why have you fasted? What would encourage you to fast on a regular basis as a spiritual discipline?

Postscript

The magi went home by another way. So also for us as we go beyond Epiphany in days to come. The gifts and abilities that brought us to the present moment will not take us forward into God's future or, as Marshall Goldsmith suggested in the title of a business book, *What Got You Here Won't Get You There*. We continue to open ourselves to the grace of God who said in a prophetic passage often read during Advent:

> I am about to do a new thing;
>   now it springs forth, do you not perceive it?
> I will make a way in the wilderness
>   and rivers in the desert. (Isa. 43:19)

Why limit these words to the season of Advent? God is always transforming the world, and transformation brings something new.

As the year moves from Epiphany to Lent and Easter, Ascension and Pentecost and the non-festival days of the year, I trust that you will remain open to the new ways of God. Practice the spiritual disciplines touched on in this book: reflection on daily Bible reading, prayer in many forms and at all times and in all places, public worship and receiving frequently the sacrament of Holy Communion, involvement in a small group for study and accountability as a disciple, fasting from food and drink or from anger or from apathy, and spiritual reading or the reading of spiritual classics.

Christian discipleship is messy. We live with a sense of God's unconditional love, and we may also struggle with a sense that we are unworthy of such love. We practice spiritual exercises diligently, and then we falter for a span in which we forget these practices. Our busy lives are full of interruptions. Yet the interruptions sometimes surprise us with moments of grace and love.

I hope the surprises that pop up in this book provide a sense of God's love in the midst of our many plans and the routine interruptions that are part of all our lives.

My South African friend Roland Rink signs many e-mails with the initials WGF: We Go Forward. In the grace and peace of God, we do go forward.

Guidance for Small Groups

You may wish to form a small group to engage in conversation about the meditations and direction in this book. Such a group may provide respite in the busyness of the Advent-Christmas-Epiphany days. If your group provides that space and nothing else, consider the group experience a blessed success. Here are some general observations about small groups:

1. Take time to talk about expectations. What do participants hope to gain from group conversation about the book? What do participants wish to receive or to give? Do you hope this group will lead to a longer group experience? Do you simply want help as you go through Advent toward Christmas?

2. Take time to learn about one another as group participants, perhaps share family background and history. You may wish to spend time in conversation about what life is like outside the church setting. Who are your friends outside the church? What are they like? What do you do beyond the congregation?

3. Take time to talk about church participation and desires for the community of faith. What is your dream for the congregation?

A Pattern for Meeting

As people gather for the group time, they will probably talk about their days. What are your personal concerns? How do you feel your faith being strengthened or being challenged during this season? Be thankful for these initial conversations.

Signal the start of group time by ringing a bell. Ring it with a sense of good cheer. You may also wish to light a candle to remind the group of God's presence. Choose someone to open the group time with prayer.

Discuss the group's readings and the questions for the week's reflections. You may wish to use questions such as the following:

- What in the meditations seemed to connect with the concerns of the world? Did any meditations go in different directions from what you expected? What did you expect?

- How did you connect with or relate to the meditations?

- What did you sense when you prayed the antiphon? How did the antiphon speak to your heart's desires?

- Did you gain a deeper sense of God's love from the readings?

- How are the meditations stirring fresh ideas in you about church ministry and mission?

After conversation about the meditations, invite participants to share aloud prayer concerns so that group members may pray for these in the days to come. Ask for a volunteer to pray for these concerns. Give thanks to God for the gift of time to gather together as a group. You may end this prayer by inviting the entire group to pray the Lord's Prayer.

After the closing prayer, extinguish the candle, ring the bell, and go about the work of preparing the way of the Lord.

Bibliography

Karl Barth. *Deliverance to the Captives*. New York: Harper & Row, Publishers, 1961.

Basil the Great. "On Fasting," *Orthodox Tradition*, vol. XXIII, no. 3, 2006. (available online <http://www.hsir.org/pdfs/2009/03/04/20090304aStBasilOnFasting%20Folder/20090304aStBasilOnFasting.pdf>

Robert Benson. *The Night of the Child*. Nashville, TN: Upper Room Books, 2001.

George Hovaness Donigian. *A World Worth Saving: Lenten Spiritual Practices for Action*. Nashville, TN: Upper Room Books, 2013.

George H. Donigian. *Three Prayers You'll Want to Pray*. New York: Church Publishing/Morehouse, 2014.

Daniel Findikyan, general editor. *The Divine Liturgy of the Armenian Church*. New York: St. Vartan Press, 2000.

George Frideric Handel. *Messiah*. Recording by Collegium Musicum 90. Oakhurst, NJ: Musical Heritage Society, 2002.

W. Paul Jones. *An Eclectic Almanac for the Faithful: People, Places, and Events That Shape Us*. Nashville, TN: Upper Room Books, 2006.

David Kherdian. *Pigs Never See the Stars: Proverbs from the Armenian*. Aurora, Oregon: Two Rivers Press, 1982.

Martin Luther. *Table Talk* (*Luther's Works*, vol. 54). Philadelphia: Fortress Press, 1967.

Jacques de Morgan. *The History of the Armenian People.* Boston, MA: Hairenik Press, 1918.

St. Grigor Narekatsi. *Speaking with God from the Depths of the Heart* (trans. by Thomas J. Samuelian). Yerevan: VEM Press, 2002. Also Krikor Naregatsi, *Lamentations,* the Armenian-language edition of Samuelian's translation. Publisher unknown. 1903. The two books are essentially the same. The variation in name shows the linguistic difference between Western Armenian and Eastern Armenian and the influence of the two different cultures that surrounded the Armenian people.

Pius Parsch. *The Church's Year of Grace* (trans. William G. Heidt). Collegeville, MN: Liturgical Press, 1959.

Sacraments and Prayers of the Armenian Church (authorized by Archbishop Torkom Manoogian). New York: Diocese of the Armenian Church of North America, 1968.

John A. Sanford. *Dreams: God's Forgotten Language.* San Francisco: Harper, 1968.

Francis Kipps Spencer. *Chrismons.* Danville, VA: Ascension Lutheran Church, 1970.

The United Methodist Book of Worship. Nashville, TN: The United Methodist Publishing House, 1992.

The United Methodist Hymnal. Nashville, TN: The United Methodist Publishing House, 1989.

Benedicta Ward. *The Sayings of the Desert Fathers: An Alphabetical Collection.* Collegeville, MN: Liturgical Press, 1984.